TWO MINUTES
IN THE BIBLE®
WITH
Jesus

BOYD BAILEY

HARVEST HOUSE PUBLISHERS
EUGENE, OREGON

Cover by Bryce Williamson

Cover image © wissanu01 / iStock

TWO MINUTES IN THE BIBLE is a trademark of Boyd Bailey. Harvest House Publishers, Inc., is the exclusive licensee of the trademark TWO MINUTES IN THE BIBLE.

TWO MINUTES IN THE BIBLE® WITH JESUS

Copyright © 2017 by Boyd Bailey
Published by Harvest House Publishers
Eugene, Oregon 97402
www.harvesthousepublishers.com

ISBN 978-0-7369-6925-3 (pbk.)
ISBN 978-0-7369-6926-0 (eBook)

Printed in the United States of America

17 18 19 20 21 22 23 24 25 / BP-GL / 10 9 8 7 6 5 4 3 2 1

To Gwynne
our very good friend
who is a lovely friend of Jesus

Acknowledgments

Thank you, Brother Marcellus from the Abbey of the Genesee outside of Rochester, New York, for being Jesus to me during a very vulnerable time in my life.

Thank you, Wisdom Hunters team, for loving the way Jesus does: Rita Bailey, Bethany Thoms, Gwynne Maffett, Shana Schutte, Rachel Snead, Rachel Prince, Tripp Prince, Susan Fox, and Josh Randolph.

Thank you, Susan Fox and Gene Skinner, for your expert editing.

Thank you, Wisdom Hunters board of directors, for your love, prayers, and accountability: Deb Ochs, Jack McEntee, Cliff Bartow, Andrew Wexler, and John Hightower.

Thank you, National Christian Foundation, for the opportunity, by God's grace, to reach and restore every person by the love of Christ, and to mobilize biblical generosity for God's kingdom.

Thank you, Harvest House Publishers, for your vision and support for this book: Bob Hawkins, Terry Glaspey, Gene Skinner, Brad Moses, Ken Lorenz, and Kathy Zemper.

Introduction

When I was a child my relationship with Jesus was rather vague and incoherent, but today we enjoy a cherished, intimate friendship. Since becoming a Christian at age 19, I've experienced an ever-growing understanding of Jesus as my Savior, Lord, and friend. Jesus is my master, whom I gladly serve—a loyal friend who is closer than a brother and, amazingly, a patient forgiver. Over and over He extends His grace in the face of my glaring sins of self-indulgence, self-reliance, and selfish withholding. My affections are easily drawn to shiny idols—pride's lies, lust's ecstasy, and greed's allure—but my jealous lover Jesus melts my heart with His uncommon mercy and grace.

These 90 writings, mostly from the four Gospels, are reflections of how Jesus loves me in spite of me, allowing perfection to relate to imperfection in a way that moves my flawed faith into closer communion with Him. Life happens every day, so my simple plan was to write about my everyday experiences, using the Gospels as a backdrop. In the process, my life intersected with Christ's life—my questions with His answers, my fears with faith in Him, my pain with Christ's comfort, my ego with His meekness, my worry with His peace, my sorrow with His joy, and my ingratitude with grateful worship of Him.

I also attempted to prayerfully understand and empathize with the hurt and hubris of Jesus's contemporaries who engaged Him at their point of need. Some, like the Roman centurion, were full of faith. Others were like the rich young ruler, who was full of himself. One leper out of ten came back to thank Jesus. One short man, Zacchaeus, was asked to open his home, where Jesus modeled how to love sinners. One woman met Jesus at a well and found living water. One adulteress met Jesus in shame, but with sensitivity He unashamedly forgave her sin and admonished her to sin no more. Jesus exposed the religious elite's hypocrisy and offered hope to the religiously inferior.

"I tell you, unless you are more right with God
than the teachers of the Law and the proud
religious law-keepers, you will never get into the
holy nation of heaven" (Matthew 5:20 NLV).

Christ's everyday encounters are eerily similar to what we encounter in our culture today. Some questions relate to money: taxes, giving, saving, and spending. Others are a bit more challenging: How do we pray like Jesus? What does it mean to follow Jesus? Is Jesus really the only way to heaven? Why are some prayers answered when others remain unanswered? How do I handle hypocrisy, forgiveness, and change? What about work, worry, war, and demons? When will Jesus return? What is God's will for my life? These are a few questions I addressed out of my own life struggles and doubts.

Our decision making can be suspect without a reliable filter to strain out the impurities and keep the purest thoughts. Just as air filters help us to breathe freely, coffee filters give us a cup of warm enjoyment, and oil filters contribute to a smooth-running engine, so asking what would Jesus have me do or not do serves as the most effective filter for making wise decisions. In light of how Jesus prayed to His Father, loved people, and approached uncertain circumstances, we must ask, what is the wisest choice? It may not be a matter of right or wrong, but of good or best. The life, death, resurrection, and teachings of Jesus provide a template of grace and truth. He is our life.

So I pray you will enjoy your journey with Jesus in these 90 readings and throughout the course of your lifetime. Keep your eyes on Him, for He will always be with you—He promised!

"I am with you always [remaining with you perpetually—
regardless of circumstance, and on every occasion],
even to the end of the age" (Matthew 28:20 AMP).

A servant and friend of Jesus,
Boyd Bailey
Roswell, Georgia

1

In Jesus's Name

Very truly I tell you, my Father will give you
whatever you ask in my name.

JOHN 16:23

At times, I find myself praying incomplete and ineffective prayers. Instead of praying in Jesus's name, I drift into praying in my name, or in the name of a cause or a church. My prayers become sterile when the spirit of my speech is self-directed, not Spirit-led. I still say "in Jesus's name," but that resembles a hollow habit or a rubber stamp instead of the Holy Spirit's validation. My prayers gain God's ear when truly I ask in Jesus's name.

In the moments preceding His passion, Jesus had the disciples' undivided attention. So He took time to remind them how to pray powerful prayers in His name. To pray in Jesus's name is to pray as a representative of the person of Christ. Pray peace because Jesus represented peace. Pray love because Jesus represented love. Pray meekness because Jesus represented meekness. Pray forgiveness because Jesus represented forgiveness. Prayers in Jesus's name are aligned with His heart. Prayers that are consistent with God's will further God's will. By faith, ask in Jesus's name.

——ᗧ∞ᗤ——

"Until now you have not asked for anything
in my name. Ask and you will receive, and
your joy will be complete" (John 16:24).

Have some of your prayers become rote and religious, lacking the Lord's leadership? One way to restore freshness in your supplications to the Savior is to write out your prayers. Put words on paper so you are precise and passionate about what stirs God's heart. Written prayers invite the Spirit to etch His desires onto the tablet of your soul. Write out what you want to live out.

You can also pray prayers found in the Bible. The precious prayers of God's people recalibrate your prayers to God's glory. "I will exalt you, my God the King" (Psalm 145:1).

There is a completeness of joy that comes from praying in Christ's name. As we pray in Jesus's name, we trust in the Lord to move hearts and accomplish His will. We rest in peace and joy, knowing He will handle whatever comes our way. Thus our sorrows become less burdensome where Jesus's joy deeply abides. Our heart can be heavy with sadness while our soul is lightened by our heavenly Father's love.

Above all, we focus on God's fame when we pray in Jesus's name. We are not the same when we pray in His name. Prayers in Jesus's name make our joy complete!

———

"Be joyful in hope, patient in affliction,
faithful in prayer" (Romans 12:12).

Heavenly Father, keep me focused on praying in Jesus's name.

Related Readings
1 Samuel 12:22; Psalm 138:2; Isaiah 56:7; Acts 4:11-12;
    Philippians 1:4

2

A Heart for God

The seed on good soil stands for those with a noble and good heart,
who hear the word, retain it, and by persevering produce a crop.

LUKE 8:15

A heart for God is nurtured by the Word of God. Just as the stomach receives good food so the body can grow, so a healthy heart receives nutritious morsels from a meal of Scripture. The spiritual development process begins with a heart hungry for God. A soft soul takes in truth and gives it time to deepen its roots in righteousness. Tests of trust come, but a humble heart stays true to its commitment to Christ. Faith perseveres and retains God's Word.

Beware of Satan's attempt to snatch away the seed from your pathway of faith and obedience. When you accept Christ by faith and obey His commands by grace, you hide the seed of God's Word from the snare of the enemy. Truth applied to your life cannot be taken by the devil. He trolls the surface of your thinking, trying to steal away the Word. However, when you hide holy Scripture deep in your heart, you are safe from the thief's clutches. You are saved!

"Samuel did not yet know the LORD: The word of the
LORD had not yet been revealed to him" (1 Samuel 3:7).

The word of the Lord allows you to know the Lord. Therefore, pace yourself in the grace of God so you continue to grow in your faith. It is not how early you start with God that counts, but how far you go over a lifetime. Don't allow trials to take away your joy in Jesus. You can still smile on the inside, even when you are suffering on the outside. The tests of your faith teach forgiveness and grace in your relationships. Life lessons empower you to love more effectively.

Cares of this world must not block us from learning the Bible and becoming better followers of Christ. Worry can keep us from the Word of God, or the Word of God can keep us from worry. Therefore, it's imperative that we quietly meditate on Scripture so the Spirit can clearly speak to our heart with reassuring words of hope, wisdom, and encouragement. Once we are rooted and grounded with a heart for God, our heavenly Father multiplies the fruit of our faith in other faithful lives.

───── ⊶⊷ ─────

"We must pay the most careful attention,
therefore, to what we have heard, so that
we do not drift away" (Hebrews 2:1).

Heavenly Father, may my humble heart be fertile ground to receive Your Word, so You can grow my faith and the faith of those I influence for You.

Related Readings

Psalm 18:30; Matthew 4:4; John 8:51; Acts 12:24; 1 Peter 1:24-25

3

Good Among Bad

———∞———

*The kingdom of heaven is like a man who sowed good seed in
his field. But while everyone was sleeping, his enemy came
and sowed weeds among the wheat, and went away.*

MATTHEW 13:24-25

God sows good seed in the world. We see the Lord's good seed all around us: churches, ministries, hospitals, orphanages, families, and individuals who love and obey Christ. Law-abiding citizens, honest taxpayers, hard workers, generous givers, and studious students all sprout from the good seed of our Savior Jesus Christ. Moreover, the sowing of God's good seed never ceases. He will raise preachers, missionaries, church planters, diplomats, and executives for His glory.

However, while God is sowing good seed around you, Satan is sowing bad seed. He is creating evil influences that seek to thwart God's plans for good. Evil will mingle with the righteous until Christ comes to separate the wheat from the tares. Thus, demon-possessed people rampage among innocent children with rapid and murderous gunfire. The sons and daughters of disobedience look for ways to steal, kill, and destroy. Bad seed grows among good.

———∞———

"You once walked according to the course of
this world, according to the prince of the power
of the air, the spirit who now works in the sons
of disobedience" (Ephesians 2:2 NKJV).

Further, the bad seed resembles the good seed, so its real nature is not revealed until it bears the fruit of its true intent. This is how two people can attend church together when one is going through the motions and the other is a dedicated disciple. You can be a church member without being a child of God. The good seed of salvation is sown along with the bad seed of hypocrisy. But we wait for Christ's judgment and pray God's grace has its transforming effect on the lost.

We are not the judge of someone's soul. God is. Yet we can model what it means to be an authentic follower of Jesus. For example, as we encounter conflict at church we can remain calm and express our concerns with a voice of reason and grace. Our role is to represent Christ in our conduct and conversation. It's the Holy Spirit's role to examine motives and expose evil intent, so we will celebrate God's sowing of good seed and prayerfully trust in Christ's judgment.

———— ∞ ————

"This will take place on the day when God judges people's secrets through Jesus Christ" (Romans 2:16).

Heavenly Father, thank You for Your good seed that grows and bears great fruit.

Related Readings

Matthew 3:12; Ephesians 5:6; 2 Timothy 4:1-2; Revelation 20:4

Fruitful Faith

———— ⚬⚬⚬ ————

Then he told this parable: "A man had a fig tree growing in his vineyard, and he went to look for fruit on it but did not find any."

LUKE 13:6

The Lord expects His children to bear fruit. A life without fruit takes up space instead of being an expression of God's grace. Our heavenly Father is patient, but He draws a line in the sand of time and says to individuals, institutions, and nations, "Repent or lose My favor." A soul or society that is barren will eventually see God move on to those governed by His principles. The fruit of faith flourishes in a heart cultivated by Christ.

What fruit is your faith producing? The fruit of peace comes after you plant the seeds of trust in Jesus. Patience's fruit appears as you prayerfully water the seeds of God's grace. The fruit of perseverance is produced when you fertilize God's goodness with faith. Humility's fruit ripens when your heavenly Father sows His loving-kindness into your soul. A harvest of good deeds—enough to fill a barn—occurs when death to self brings your love to life!

———— ⚬⚬⚬ ————

"I [Jesus] am the true vine, and my Father is the
gardener. He cuts off every branch in me that bears no
fruit, while every branch that does bear fruit he prunes
so that it will be even more fruitful" (John 15:1-2).

The mercy of the Lord does include a pruning process. Instead of immediately removing a fruitless faith, He gives it time to grow by the shears of suffering. Yes, pain is meant to purge us from unhealthy habits and remind us of our undeniable dependence on Christ. Our heavenly husbandman cuts back our branches diseased by sin. Jesus, our vine of spiritual nutrients, feeds our faith. Then the Holy Spirit nurtures the blossoms in our life, known as the fruit of the Spirit.

If the compassionate and thorough work of the Trinity is ignored, we are in danger of being cut off from the life-giving grace of the Father, Son, and Spirit. As believers we are commanded by Christ to spread the manure of His mercy around the base of the unhealthy lives we influence. Yes, our service may smell repulsive to sinful souls, but our relentless love and forgiveness may facilitate fruit with the sweet aroma of salvation. Fruitful faith enjoys God's favor.

"The one who plants and the one who waters have one purpose, and they will each be rewarded according to their own labor" (1 Corinthians 3:8).

Heavenly Father, prune my unhealthy attitudes and actions, so I can serve others.

Related Readings
Isaiah 5:2; Jeremiah 8:13; John 15:5-8; Hebrews 6:7

Friendship with Jesus

You are my friends if you do what I command.

JOHN 15:14

J esus is a friend to His followers. He is Lord, but He is a friend. He is
Savior, but He is a friend. He is the Son of God, but He is a friend.
He is sinless and holy, but He is a friend. He is a friend to sinners,
and a friend to those He saves. Jesus is a friend to His followers, but
it is a friendship based on obedience. Complying with Christ creates
companionship.

If I do not obey Christ's commands, He does not call me friend.
It is through our actions that friendship with Jesus is validated. Obedience to Jesus inspires intimacy with Him. In obeying Jesus, we can
really get to know Him. His friendship is free for all who follow hard
with a heart hungry to obey. Friendship flourishes with faithful fidelity.

"Blessed rather are those who hear the
word of God and obey it" (Luke 11:28).

Friendship with Jesus is an invitation to intimacy. He reveals to His
friends the riches of His grace and the hope of His glory. It is a friendship that bears the fruit of saved souls and solid character. You begin to
emulate the attitude, actions, words, and spirit of Jesus, because this
is what friends do. Friends look, act, and sound like each other. You
know you are a friend of Jesus when Jesus consistently influences you
to be like Him.

When others are around you, does your behavior provide evidence
that you've been with Jesus? Is it a friendship based on conviction, not
convenience; intimacy, not intimidation; and giving, not getting? As

you grow in your friendship with Christ, you better understand His heart, and your prayers align more with His will. Friendship with Jesus facilitates friendship with people. True friends flock to be with fellow friends of Jesus. Evangelism of the lost and edification of the saved flow freely when Jesus is your best friend.

———∞∞∞———

"When Jesus saw their faith, he said, 'Friend, your sins are forgiven'" (Luke 5:20).

How can I enjoy my friendship with Jesus and also honor Him in the process?

Related Readings
2 Chronicles 20:7; Job 29:4; James 2:23; 4:4

6

Little to Big

Then Jesus asked, "What is the kingdom of God like? What shall I compare it to? It is like a mustard seed, which a man took and planted in his garden. It grew and became a tree, and the birds perched in its branches."

LUKE 13:18-19

The Lord loves to take a little and make it big for His kingdom's purposes. He takes a little faith in His provision and produces an ongoing supply, possibly even surplus. He takes a little love of family and grows a lasting legacy for the Lord. He takes little financial investments and compounds them into recurring support for those who steward consistently and wisely. He takes a little obedience and multiplies His influence globally. He takes a little vision and grows it into a God-sized idea.

However, to grow something for God takes disciplined faith and obedience on our part. We can't quit in the middle of the maturation process; otherwise, we miss out on the Lord's lasting outcome. Just as a beautiful baby takes nine months to reach full term, so the blessings of God gestate by grace, mature by prayerful obedience, and are birthed by trust in His timing. Thus, we stay in the process with Jesus. In His good time, He grows our big vision to bring Him glory!

"You need to persevere so that when you
have done the will of God, you will receive
what he has promised" (Hebrews 10:36).

Will you run away when things get rough? Or will you stay in the game by God's grace? Anyone can quit, and few are faithful. The process is as important as the progress and the end product. Therefore, stay engaged with Jesus and enjoy Him as you journey through stages of life. Your consistent acts of obedience, as little as they might seem, lead to the Lord's bigger opportunities.

Most of all, take a little time each day to spend with your heavenly Father. The taproot of your trust in God deepens and expands, so the trunk of your life becomes like a broad and bold sequoia. The sturdy branches of your beliefs are a safe place to sit and rest for those who need the sanctuary of your encouragement. Yes, you may have started with an acorn of salvation, but God will grow you into His bigger oak tree of blessing. Grace keeps you growing in Him!

⸺ ∽∾∽ ⸺

> "Grow in the grace and knowledge of our Lord and Savior Jesus Christ. To him be glory both now and forever! Amen" (2 Peter 3:18).

Heavenly Father, grow me into Your big blessing for those I meet day to day.

Related Readings

Matthew 17:20; Luke 17:6; 2 Corinthians 2:14; Colossians 1:6

7

Walk with Jesus

Yet you have a few people in Sardis who have not soiled their clothes.
They will walk with me, dressed in white, for they are worthy.

REVELATION 3:4

Three or four times a week Rita and I walk together in our hilly neighborhood. Our purpose is not to train for an Ironman, but to increase our heart rate and decrease our stress. On the level stretches or when we gingerly step downhill, we take turns talking about the best and worst parts of our week. Our conversation tends to complement real hurts with hopeful healing. We discuss (sometimes debate) topics such as financial management and calendar coordination. We walk together so we can share and better understand each other.

John, the Apostle of Love, compliments the few among the church in Sardis who have remained pure in the face of impure peer pressure. This remnant was just enough spiritual salt to preserve a dying body of believers. The church in Sardis was not persecuted because it was in a spiritual coma. Scripturally incoherent and void of prayer, these church attenders were not a threat to the enemy's strategy to silence the church, but the few who really knew God walked with Jesus.

"If we walk in the light, as he is in the light, we have fellowship with one another, and the blood of Jesus, his Son, purifies us from all sin" (1 John 1:7).

Is your walk with the Lord contingent upon circumstances, or does it transcend all situations? It's not enough to just go to God when the going gets tough. Your spiritual health needs attention at all times. Consistently walk with Jesus on the level stretches of life. Hold His hand on the downhill steps of success—then you will be better prepared to persevere in prayer while climbing up the steep hills of adversity. During treacherous ascents—Christ, the experienced mountain climber—pulls you up by the secure ropes of radical trust. Perseverance requires one step of faith at a time.

You are God's seasoning for the salvation of souls. Some within your church congregation are not saved. You are planted by the Holy Spirit to be a loving reminder as an authentic follower of Jesus. Your greatest mission field may be those you worship with on Sunday morning. Look for opportunities to initiate friendships. Invite acquaintances into a small group to study the Bible. Walk with others through life, so they can grow in their walk with Jesus.

———◦◦◦———

"On the day he comes to be glorified in his holy
people and to be marveled at among all those
who have believed" (2 Thessalonians 1:10).

Dear Jesus, I desire to walk with You through the ups, downs, and level stretches of life.

Related Readings
Genesis 5:24; Joshua 22:5; Luke 24:15; 2 Corinthians 12:18

8

Change Agent

---

*Again he asked, "What shall I compare the kingdom of God
to? It is like yeast that a woman took and mixed into about
sixty pounds of flour until it worked all through the dough."*

LUKE 13:20-21

The word of Christ is a change agent for the kingdom of God. Like small batches of yeast, truth leavens the Lord's influence in a heart and soul. A little bit of Scripture goes a long way toward growing a quickened heart for the Lord. The firm but loving fingers of our heavenly Father work the yeast of His love into our pliable soul. Patience sees faith rise up and cause a life to become appetizing, like the aroma of fresh baked bread. Truth is a change agent for the soul.

Furthermore, it takes work to knead the yeast of Yahweh into a life. The Holy Spirit is like the diligent cook who works the dough with beauty and persistence. The dough of our soul is tossed and turned, pounded and made smooth, so the yeast of God's love works its influence into our inner being. We feel unstable at times, but this trusting posture invites us to receive faith's full effects. Yes, faith's fermenting process grows a bold and robust belief. A little leaven transforms.

"A little yeast works through the whole
batch of dough" (Galatians 5:9).

Therefore, keep your heart softened with humility and pliable with prayer. A hard piece of dough is unable to grow, but a heart full of grace submits to the Holy Spirit's control. Each day is an opportunity for Christ to bake fresh bread from our available life. Moldy and hardened bread is thrown out, fit only for the trash, but fresh bread is the dinner table centerpiece for all to anticipate. Is your life an opportunity for Almighty God? The Bread of Life changes you into His bread of life.

Lastly, be aware of unseemly influences that subtly change your heart's desires. There is bad yeast, so beware! The yeast of greed quits growing generosity. The yeast of cynicism quits growing faith. The yeast of selfishness quits growing service. Thus, the best remedy for bad yeast is to replace it with the good yeast of God. Invite Christ to be your change agent for Him. Daily, kneel before your heavenly Father, so He can knead His character into your softened heart!

—◦◦◦—

"Your boasting is not good. Don't you know that a little yeast leavens the whole batch of dough?" (1 Corinthians 5:6).

Heavenly Father, keep my heart softened by humility, so You can knead into my life what I need from You.

Related Readings

Exodus 13:3; Matthew 16:6; John 6:33; 1 Corinthians 5:7

9

Only Way to God

*Thomas said to him, "Lord, we don't know where you are going,
so how can we know the way?"
Jesus answered, "I am the way and the truth and the life.
No one comes to the Father except through me."*

JOHN 14:5-6

The only way to God is through faith in Jesus Christ. There is one path to the Almighty, and it's through His Son. Any add-ons to trust in Christ replace faith alone as the gateway to God. The route to our heavenly Father is not Jesus plus religious fervor. The faith journey to heaven is not Jesus plus denominational loyalty. Becoming a Christian is not Christ plus a compelling cause. Jesus Christ is God. When introduced to Jesus we are introduced to God.

Thomas voiced the disciples' concerns, doubts, and fears. They had experienced the truth of Jesus's life-changing and life-giving teaching, but they still lacked the comprehension of why He must die. Though they saw Jesus raise Lazarus from the dead, they still did not understand that after three days Christ would rise from the grave. Jesus's death would allow them to experience the living Lord. The way to God is made clear when we accept Jesus as God.

*"No one has ever seen God, but the one
and only Son [Jesus], who is himself God
and is in closest relationship with the Father,
has made him known" (John 1:18).*

Do you believe Jesus is only a manifestation of God—or God manifest? Are you trusting in anyone or anything other than Jesus Christ to get you to God? Start by loving Him with your heart. By faith receive Jesus into your heart. Allow His free-flowing grace to forgive you of your sin. Embrace Him and His unconditional love. Now love Him with your mind. Believe Jesus is God. Trust that He is the only way to your heavenly Father. Love God with your soul. Rest in His peace and security. Lastly, love God by submitting your will to His will.

Furthermore, as a disciple of Jesus, make it a priority to show and tell others how and why He is the only way to God. Like His followers after His resurrection, we cannot keep quiet since the Holy Spirit has quieted our soul and filled us with holy boldness! By grace we remain faithful to Christ: the Way, the Truth, and the Life. We know Him, so we can make Him known. Jesus is the only way to God.

"Salvation is found in no one else, for there is
no other name under heaven given to mankind
by which we must be saved" (Acts 4:12).

Heavenly Father, thanks for making belief in Jesus the way to You.

Related Readings

John 10:9; Ephesians 2:18; 1 Timothy 2:5; Hebrews 10:20

10

Hidden Treasure

The kingdom of heaven is like treasure hidden in a field.
When a man found it, he hid it again, and then in his
joy went and sold all he had and bought that field.

MATTHEW 13:44

Followers of Jesus have the joy and privilege of treasuring God. Like an archaeologist for the Almighty, they dig in the dirt of His love and are surprised by His generosity with the precious metals of grace and truth. Jesus is the preeminent jewel. When excavated from this field of faith, He invites us to a lifetime of discovery and renewal. Indeed, searching for spiritual treasure requires trust and persistence. So, enjoy the process that produces character in sincere seekers.

Are you motivated to make kingdom priorities your number one goal? Are you intentional in seeking intimacy with Jesus? To be sure, it feels laborious at times, but your labor is not in vain. Once you are converted to Christ, resolve to hide the truth of God in your heart, and in the process position your life to be leveraged for the Lord. Your sold-out life reflects a beautiful orchard for all to admire its Creator—Christ. Work in fields of faith that yield massive, good fruit.

"My goal is that they may...know the mystery of God,
namely, Christ, in whom are hidden all the treasures
of wisdom and knowledge" (Colossians 2:2-3).

We have the unique opportunity and stewardship to seek out the wisdom and knowledge of God in Christ. A good step is to process our findings in prayer and meditation. Like a California gold miner we pan for God's gold nuggets with our wire filter of Scripture, which separates fool's gold from wisdom's gold. In what can be a monotonous discipline we will find a variety of gold treasure: dustings of discernment, slivers of hope, nuggets of wisdom, and rocks of faith.

When you decide to sell out for Jesus, He may very well require you to sell off some or all of your stuff for kingdom investments. Complexity is the enemy retaining an eternal perspective, while simplicity is a friend who facilitates kingdom outcomes. Thus, pray about how to use your worldly assets to send ahead for your heavenly reward. Surround yourself with seasoned mentors who model investing in spiritual treasures. Yes, create kingdom wealth, lasting now and forever!

"If you look for [wisdom] as for silver
and search for it as hidden treasure,
then you will understand the fear of the LORD
and find the knowledge of God" (Proverbs 2:4-5).

Heavenly Father, I commit to seek intimacy with my Savior Jesus to hide Your truth in my heart.

Related Readings

Psalm 105:3; Isaiah 12:3; Luke 12:34; John 5:39-40; 1 Timothy 6:19

11

The Pearl of Great Price

*Again, the kingdom of heaven is like a merchant looking
for fine pearls. When he found one of great value, he went
away and sold everything he had and bought it.*

MATTHEW 13:45-46

What is the pearl of great price? Simply Jesus. He is the only One worth selling everything you have to follow by faith. God made His children spiritual merchants on a quest for what's most valuable in life. These earnest explorations of religion are empty, until the grace of God in Jesus Christ is uncovered and understood. Vain treasures are those mini pearls that are but a weak reflection of the genuine One. Sincere efforts to search out the most significant asset of God will find Christ.

There are many fine pearls that draw our attention away from the pearl of great price, Jesus. The pearl of pride draws us away, toward our own limited abilities. The flashy pearl of entertainment consumes our energy and dulls our senses. The pearl of religious hypocrisy creates an image without any spiritual substance. And the black pearl of unbelief keeps us from experiencing God. But, as we enjoy the Great Pearl in an intimate relationship, we need no more.

"It is because of him that you are in Christ
Jesus, who has become for us wisdom from
God—that is, our righteousness, holiness
and redemption" (1 Corinthians 1:30).

How do you steward your greatest asset from Almighty God? What disciplines are you developing to not take for granted your most valued resource? One way to value your most valuable belonging is to share it with others. It can't be weakened by too much use. It can't be ignored while on display in your life. You are truly wealthy when you are graced by the riches of God, but you are utterly poor and spiritually bankrupt without engaging the Great Pearl of Christ.

Lastly, sell or give away whatever is necessary to enjoy your riches in Christ. Your cluttered life can easily leave out the Lord. The complexity of stuff can cause you to miss the simplicity in Christ. Streamline your schedule so you have time for intimacy with your heavenly Father, and your relational engagement with those you love. Jesus Christ is your Pearl. So value Him greatly by giving Him your full love and devotion!

—∞—

"For you know the grace of our Lord Jesus Christ,
that though he was rich, yet for your sake he
became poor, so that you through his poverty
might become rich" (2 Corinthians 8:9).

Heavenly Father, I am grateful for the riches I have in Your Son Jesus Christ.

Related Readings
Proverbs 22:2; Matthew 7:6; Romans 2:4; Ephesians 1:7; Revelation 3:17

12

Prepare for Jesus

———— ⚬⚬⚬ ————

She gave birth to her firstborn, a son. She wrapped
him in cloths and placed him in a manger, because
there was no guest room available for them.

LUKE 2:7

The preparation for our first baby was exciting and scary. Exciting, because of the anticipation of enjoying God's gift of life in a little one like us. Scary, because we had never been parents before. She came with no instruction manual (the Bible of course), but there was so much we didn't know. We thought we were somewhat ready on that cold rainy day in November, but we had much to learn. Parental preparation got us so far, but our experience tested our assumptions.

Joseph and Mary prepared as best they could, but they faced unfriendly circumstances. Crowded travel to another town with no place to stay put pressure on their faith and physical stamina. Even more disturbing was the community's lack of interest in Christ's coming. Some came from afar to honor Him, but fewer close by celebrated the birth of their Lord and Savior Jesus. Not many were prepared for Jesus. He came to give life, but began life corralled in the corner of a barn. His audience was lowly beasts incapable of belief. Jesus deserves our proper preparation.

———— ⚬⚬⚬ ————

"A voice of one calling:
'In the wilderness prepare
the way for the LORD;
make straight in the desert
a highway for our God'" (Isaiah 40:3).

How can we prepare for Jesus in our hearts and in our homes? Our humble hearts offer the best hospitality for our Lord and Savior Jesus. He is at home where confession of sin comforts the soul and brings inner contentment. We prepare our hearts for Jesus by keeping them pure. Moreover, our homes grow peaceful as we develop a culture of prayer. We pray at home together and we pray as we go about our day-to-day activities. Families who prepare for Jesus invite His thinking into their conversations. Read together the words of Christ and apply them to your life.

We plan ways to become more loving and generous, because of the great love and gift of God in His Son Jesus Christ. We know we have prepared for Jesus when we have received Jesus. Have you given your all over to Him? What area of your life needs Christ's Lordship? Yes, life is a continual preparation for what God has next. Trust Him with eternal life, so you can trust Him with life on earth. Prepare for Jesus— He is coming again soon!

"He who testifies to these things says, 'Yes, I am coming soon.' Amen. Come, Lord Jesus" (Revelation 22:20).

Heavenly Father, prepare me to receive everything You have for me in Christ Jesus.

Related Readings

Isaiah 9:6; Micah 5:2; John 1:11; 1 John 5:20

13

Hypocrites Exposed

⚬⚬⚬

*This is how it will be at the end of the age. The angels will come and
separate the wicked from the righteous and throw them into the
blazing furnace, where there will be weeping and gnashing of teeth.*

MATTHEW 13:49-50

There are posers who profess to know God, but He will one day
say to them, "I never knew you." It is scary to think an individual can believe they are okay with the Lord when they are not. Maybe
they heard the truth of the cross, but they did not receive the truth by
faith into their heart. There has not been an exchange of trust in themselves to a total dependence on Christ. Fools may have good religious
feelings, but they have not trusted in Jesus alone.

Have you truly trusted Jesus as your Lord and Savior? Is your love
and affection captured by the love of your heavenly Father? If not, it
is wise to be circumspect about your commitment to Christ. As Jesus
stated, mingling with the good fish does not make you a good fish. A
bad fish smells like a fish, looks like a fish, and tastes like a fish, but it
remains in its original state until it's drawn to heaven by God. Make
sure the scales of sin are removed from your spiritual eyes.

⚬⚬⚬

"Immediately, something like scales fell from
Saul's eyes, and he could see again. He
got up and was baptized" (Acts 9:18).

It is uncomfortable to picture a loving God having a system of judgment that includes hell. However, would He really be loving if He did
not punish sin and expose religious hypocrites for pretending to be
true followers of Jesus? We water down the Word of God when we

feel like we have to apologize for the Lord's consequences that accompany improper beliefs. Oh how He loves us, because on Judgment Day, wrongs will be made right in His sight.

Therefore, in the meantime, pray for those who genuinely believe they are right with God but have yet to be born again. Teach those who are religious but lost about a desperate desire for the Lord that follows submission to the Lord. Help fellow church members move from a head full of knowledge to a heart full of passion to pray. Information about Jesus becomes alive when you experience Jesus in a personal, loving, and intimate relationship. Better a hypocrite's exposure now, than later.

—∞∞—

"If you declare with your mouth, 'Jesus is Lord,' and believe in your heart that God raised him from the dead, you will be saved" (Romans 10:9).

Heavenly Father, lead me into a genuine relationship with You through Your Son Jesus.

Related Readings
Matthew 7:21; 25:32; Romans 14:11; 1 Corinthians 14:21; Revelation 20:15

14

Count the Costs

*In the same way, those of you who do not give
up everything cannot be my disciples.*

LUKE 14:33

Abandonment is the attitude of disciples of Jesus Christ. Utter abandonment to fame, fortune, friends, and family to carry out Christ's calling. I don't like these hard words of Jesus, but they are a test of my true love for Him. Am I a casual Christian, or am I a committed Christian? Motivations of convenience and comfort bear the fruit of shallow spirituality while the desire of death to self bears the fruit of unencumbered obedience. Count the costs before commitment.

Zealous fools begin but do not proceed down the path of the Lord's purposes for their life. However, as a sober-minded disciple who counted the costs, you answered Christ's call to follow Him. Your commitment was based on the courage and resolution to do the next right thing, regardless. The gates of hell do not prevail, because you are executing God's game plan. You have a visceral sense of destiny because you are following the most trusted One, Jesus. He is worth it!

—◇◇◇—

"Watch out that you do not lose what we have worked
for, but that you may be rewarded fully" (2 John 1:8).

Furthermore, tribulation and persecution will come when we persistently love and serve in Jesus's name. The outside forces of radical resistance are not meant to be met with our radical activism. A combative and harsh religion loses its attractiveness. Thus, when we feel pressure to conform to the culture, we invite the Holy Spirit to conform us into the likeness of Jesus. He raises the stakes with our radical love, forgiveness, acceptance, and service.

Have you given up everything for God, only to experience His generous return policy? All we have is His anyway, but our gracious heavenly Father allows us to steward His assets. What we desperately hold on to, He often takes and gives away. What we freely let go of, He may give back if we can be trusted with His blessings. Therefore, count the costs as a Christ follower by being a radical doer of the Word. Be known by how well you love. Give up everything for Him!

"I consider everything a loss because of the
surpassing worth of knowing Christ Jesus my Lord,
for whose sake I have lost all things. I consider them
garbage, that I may gain Christ" (Philippians 3:8).

Heavenly Father, my heart is to die to self and to live for You.

Related Readings

Psalm 73:25; Jeremiah 9:23-24; Romans 8:36; 1 Corinthians 15:31

15

Love Initiates

――――――∞∞――――――

*Suppose one of you has a hundred sheep and loses one
of them. Doesn't he leave the ninety-nine in the open
country and go after the lost sheep until he finds it?*

LUKE 15:4

Love takes the lead in looking out for the needs of another. Grace
is a prayerful process of anticipating how someone may be hurting or feeling insecure in their loneliness. Love does not wait until a
suffering soul solicits relief; rather, compassion is a cure in search of a
wounded spirit. Friends or family may wander away to do their own
thing, but love keeps up with them. Mercy connects creatively with a
cavalier comrade. Love leaves the many to care for the one.

Is one person really worth our effort? Absolutely! Jesus died for us
as individuals. A schoolmate or relative probably reached out to us
when we were outside the faith. Yes, our prayers for a single soul need
to be followed up with expressions of their worth to God and to us.
Your love is irresistible in its effect on those lured into the world's system. Thus, give without expecting anything in return, and you will see
some return to their Savior. Go love for God.

――――――∞∞――――――

"For this is what the Sovereign LORD says:
I myself will search for my sheep and
look after them" (Ezekiel 34:11).

Moreover, your heavenly Father is relentless in His love for you. Sin
may have scattered you to the fringes of His green pastures, but He still
desires you. Your soul may feel distant from faith's security, and if so,
surrender to your Great Shepherd's care. If your confidence is crippled,

let Christ lift you in His arms of love and carry you back to the care of His faith community. The Lord of the universe is concerned about your one concern, so cast your cares on Your Lover.

Above all, receive the love of the Lord and the love of others. Pride resists help, but humility invites support from Jesus and His followers. Love retained is hope regained. Other green pastures beyond the fence posts of faith are a fallacy. Nothing can compete with Christ's love. Allow Him to shepherd your soul through anger, conflict, rejection, and disrespect. Your heavenly Father initiates love for you, so you can propagate His love to lost people. Love initiates!

"He will stand and shepherd his flock
in the strength of the LORD,
in the majesty of the name of the LORD his God.
And they will live securely" (Micah 5:4).

Heavenly Father, thanks for pursuing me when I drift away from Your love and care.

Related Readings
Psalms 23:1-6; 119:176; Jeremiah 31:10; Luke 19:10; Hebrews 13:16

Heartfelt Forgiveness

*This is how my heavenly Father will treat each of you unless
you forgive your brother or sister from your heart.*

MATTHEW 18:35

Forgiveness is a serious matter to our heavenly Father. It is so significant that He gave His only Son, Jesus, on a cruel cross as forgiveness for our sins. Forgiveness wipes clean a debt that was humanly impossible to pay: only the sinless One can forgive sin. Because of God's monumental mercy on us, He expects us to extend this unconditional grace to our offenders. Gratitude has a long memory of His great grace. We forgive freely because God, for Christ's sake, has forgiven us!

Our heartfelt forgiveness gives us freedom. It frees us to be who God wants us to be. Forgiveness frees us from the need to pay back or heap guilt and condemnation on the one who hurt us. When we let go of anger, even bitterness, our emotional energy is free to comfort and care for the needs of other searching souls. A heart bound up in its own hurt cannot even care for itself. Indeed, forgiveness shifts our focus from the idol of self-pity to the praise of God in His mercy.

"For if you forgive other people when they sin against
you, your heavenly Father will also forgive you. But
if you do not forgive others their sins, your Father
will not forgive your sins" (Matthew 6:14-15).

You sin when you choose not to forgive. Furthermore, your fellowship with your heavenly Father is stifled without your heartfelt forgiveness. Your intimacy erodes without the clean slate of forgiveness from Christ. So, how can you know if you have truly forgiven someone who has hurt, even violated you? You begin to bless them instead of curse them. You talk well about them behind their back. You pray for them to grow in God's grace. Forgiveness frees you to love well.

There is a risk involved in your heartfelt forgiveness. Your offender may continue their disrespectful, potentially harmful behavior. They may take advantage of your goodwill. Your forgiveness is no guarantee they will change, but you will change. Christ will conform you into His work of grace, mercy, and love. God will deal with the unruly ones in His timing. Their conscience, the Holy Spirit's auditor, will bring them into account. Your heartfelt forgiveness reveals God's heart.

"Bear with each other and forgive one another if any of you has a grievance against someone. Forgive as the Lord forgave you" (Colossians 3:13).

Heavenly Father, Your great forgiveness compels me to forgive freely.

Related Readings

Luke 6:37; Ephesians 4:2; 4:32; Colossians 2:14; James 2:13

Belonging to Jesus

⌒∞⌒

*Paul, an apostle of Christ Jesus by the will of God, to God's
holy people in Ephesus, the faithful in Christ Jesus.*

EPHESIANS 1:1

I belong to Jesus Christ. He is the owner of my life, the master of my eternal fate, and the focus of my devotion. It's a daily battle to fight off competing owners of my life: the world, the flesh, and the devil. Like a rogue activist investor who tries to take over a company, unseemly forces other than faith vie for my allegiance. I have to remind myself to whom I belong and what He wants for me.

Paul is writing to a group of Christians in Ephesus who faced the challenge of competing loyalties. The love of money, immoral deception, worldly worship, and sin's allure all recruited members into their belief system. In some ways modern culture looks tame compared to the openly iniquitous and secular society of the Ephesians. Yet Paul highlighted those holy believers in Christ Jesus, who were set apart for Him. Holiness begins with our proximity of belonging to God—for God. All are saints who trust in Christ alone.

⌒∞⌒

"Though you have not seen him, you love
him; and even though you do not see him
now, you believe in him and are filled with an
inexpressible and glorious joy" (1 Peter 1:8).

Security comes to those secure in their Savior Jesus. Because we are owned by God, no other prospectors can claim Christ's claim on us. Our heavenly Father has the deed to our souls, and no one and nothing has the authority to take us away from Him. Our soul's title insurance is trust in Jesus. The more we rest in God's ownership of our life—the more we are filled with inexpressible joy. Faith is a fortress for our joy's protection from anxious warriors.

Furthermore, where we belong is what we become. Just as members of a club tend to take on the traits of other club members, so we become more like Christ as we understand and apply our membership of faith. We pay our dues in daily devotion of love for our Lord and people. We move from duty to delight the more we delight in God's ownership over us. Christianity is not a compartment that contains the religious part of our life. Christ is our life. What He owns—He takes care of. We become like Jesus—because we belong to Jesus!

"So, my brothers and sisters, you also died to the law through the body of Christ, that you might belong to another, to him who was raised from the dead, in order that we might bear fruit for God" (Romans 7:4).

Heavenly Father, because I belong to You—I want to become like You.

Related Readings
Romans 8:9; 12:5; 1 Corinthians 15:23; 2 Corinthians 10:7; Galatians 5:24

18

Cause for Celebration

———— ∞ ————

*In the same way, I tell you, there is rejoicing in the presence
of the angels of God over one sinner who repents.*

LUKE 15:10

The great God of the universe and those in the presence of angels
rejoice when a single sinner repents. A conversion to Christ is a
big, big deal to the Lord. As a body healed of disease celebrates wholeness, a soul healed of sin's terminal illness can't help but bring glory to
God in celebratory praise. What was lost is found. What was estranged
from the Holy Spirit is unified with God's Spirit. What was sentenced
to hell is pardoned for heaven. New life deserves a party!

Do you make a special effort to recognize a friend or relative's decision to trust Christ? Perhaps you attend their baptism, buy them a
Bible, or lead them through a discipleship process for new believers.
Maybe you throw a party with a delicious meal and a time of affirmation for the one who has passed from death to life. Just as we lavish
care and attention upon a physical birth, so time and money are great
investments in a new birth. Celebrate a new Christian's faith!

———— ∞ ————

"Glory to God in the highest heaven, and on earth
peace to those on whom his favor rests" (Luke 2:14).

Be intentional not to take for granted someone who, by grace,
engaged God for the very first time. A faith that becomes too familiar
with itself is a tired faith. However, a faith fired by the flames of a fresh
faith is energized and reminded of its past zeal. Oh the joy of being a
spiritual parent and grandparent. Alive and well are disciples who are

blessed to experience a soul's new creation within relationships they love. Yes, there is no greater joy than serving as a spiritual midwife.

Our heavenly Father throws a party for those who have come home to Christ. He laughs and sings songs of jubilation when His children repent of foolish living and turn to trust in Him. He expects His other children to join Him in a euphoric expression of gratitude over one sinner who has come to their senses. A saved soul is extremely valuable in eternity's currency. Like a found silver coin on earth, is a converted soul in heaven. A conversion to Christ is cause for rejoicing!

———∞∞∞———

"I have no greater joy than to hear that my
children are walking in the truth" (3 John 1:4).

Heavenly Father, I rejoice with You over those who have come to faith in Jesus.

Related Readings

Psalms 51:12; 95:1; Isaiah 65:14; Daniel 12:3; 1 John 2:1

19

Moral Police

*The older brother became angry and refused to go in. So his father went
out and pleaded with him. But he answered his father, "Look! All
these years I've been slaving for you and never disobeyed your orders."*

LUKE 15:28-29

Some religious people feel responsible for monitoring others' behavior with moral smugness. They judge people's motives, while their own heart becomes filled with a sense of superiority. These defenders of their definition of decency feel no need for mercy, nor do they offer mercy. The Bible becomes a "billy club" to whip people into shape with bouts of shame and guilt. Ironically, moral police lack moral authority. Their pronouncements are birthed from pride, not pity.

The moral police are driven by anger. They are not satisfied until everyone they know conforms to their standards. They become especially perturbed when a sinner repents and is accepted back into the fold of faith. Cynically they say, "Is his conversion real?" "If anyone deserves recognition and rewards for their behavior, I do, because I have always been a good person." Indeed, their pious prayers preach down to those less religious. They become a closed-minded judge and jury.

"But to Jonah this seemed very wrong, and
he became angry...But the LORD replied, 'Is it
right for you to be angry?'" (Jonah 4:1,4).

Has your religious zeal drifted into the arrogant attitude of the older brother in Jesus's story: jealous, judgmental, and joyless? Are you bound up within because life doesn't seem to listen to your demands?

The same Lord you represent can free you from being a self-appointed judge. Take a step off your religious pedestal of pride and kneel in humble brokenness. Confess the need to be free from an attitude of moral superiority and admit to being a chief of sinners.

The moral police of Jesus's day had Him crucified. Today we are called to be crucified with Christ, so we are reminded of our weak condition outside the love and grace of God. Yes, there are standards God expects us to obey. Christ calls us to a high level of moral and ethical behavior. However, it is the inner work of the Spirit that conforms us into the image of Christ. Truth transforms us from the inside out, so we walk in humility not pride. God is our judge.

"Don't pick on people, jump on their failures, criticize their faults—unless, of course, you want the same treatment. That critical spirit has a way of boomeranging" (Matthew 7:1-2 MSG).

Heavenly Father, forgive me for judging others and neglecting my own proud heart.

Related Readings

Luke 6:41-42; Romans 14:10; 1 Corinthians 4:5; 5:12; James 4:11

Living in the Present Is a Present

*Pay attention to how you hear. To those who listen to
my teaching, more understanding will be given.*

LUKE 8:18 NLT

Recently a friend took me to lunch. His agenda? To hear how I was doing. What a gift! For more than an hour Bill just wanted me to talk about what the Lord was teaching me, how my family was doing, and how he could pray for me. His phone was nowhere to be seen or heard, his eye contact was riveting, and his emotional engagement was energizing. My special friend gave me the gift of his uninterrupted presence. A gift of love!

Jesus taught compellingly about the importance of truly paying attention and listening to the life lessons found in His teachings. Because He illustrated truth with everyday examples, clearer comprehension was available. But the deepest understanding only came to those who were intellectually, spiritually, physically, and emotionally engaged in hearing what Christ had to say. For believers, being present in the presence of Jesus is not passive prayer, but proactive listening. The heart hears best when it has been cleansed by the Spirit and eagerly communes with Christ.

"I delight in your instructions.
My suffering was good for me,
for it taught me to pay attention to your
decrees" (Psalm 119:70-71 NLT).

Suffering can be the Spirit's megaphone to speak to our spirit. When we become too busy with our business, the Lord knows how to slow us down so we pay attention to *His* business. Instead of pushing through a sickness, maybe we take a few days off—rest—and be present with our heavenly Father. Better to learn what the Lord is attempting to say through a small setback, than be sidelined for a significant period of time—and be forced to give God our focused presence.

Who hungers for you to be all there when you are with them? A spouse, child, friend, or work associate? Being truly present is the fruit of trust. You trust other responsibilities can wait, and by taking a break from obsessing over critical issues, you can reengage, invigorated with new and better insight. By investing 100 percent of your attention in a conversation with a coworker, you can trust the Lord is at work in ways all around you. He is moving the hearts of authorities and procuring resources to support your opportunities. Trust that God is presently at work!

―∞∞―

"My child, pay attention to what I say.
Listen carefully to my words.
Do not lose sight of them.
Let them penetrate deep into your
heart" (Proverbs 4:20-21 NLT).

Heavenly Father, I want to trust You 100 percent so I can give the gift of my 100 percent presence.

Related Readings
Psalms 16:11; 34:11-16; Acts 2:28; 1 Timothy 6:12

21

Place of Torment

I beg you, father, send Lazarus to my family, for I
have five brothers. Let him warn them, so that they
will not also come to this place of torment.

LUKE 16:27-28

There is a place of torment designated for those who die without trusting in Jesus Christ as their Lord and Savior. It is a lonely
place void of the Lord's presence and His loving comfort. No courier
can be sent from the other side to warn those on this side. A decision
to follow Jesus must be made on earth to gain a future place in heaven.
Those who reject the Lord before they die will be rejected after they die,
but salvation from a tormented soul is certain through faith in Christ.

Life on earth is only a brief prelude to our eternal existence. The
proud will strut across life's stage concerned only for themselves. The
humble bow in dependence on Christ, prepared to meet their Maker
after death's final curtain comes down. Only fools follow the path of
the devil and his demons. Yes, evil on earth is compounded in eternity
outside the influence of Holy God. The place of torment is no place
for those who have placed their total trust in Jesus.

꧀

"It has now been revealed through the appearing
of our Savior, Christ Jesus, who has destroyed
death and has brought life and immortality to
light through the gospel" (2 Timothy 1:10).

Have riches kept you from a real relationship with Jesus Christ?
Are you warning friends and family members today of the judgment
to come outside of Christ? Yes, we are to engage lost loved ones with

eternal truths wrapped in our care and concern. We love others at their point of emotional, physical, and financial need so we can share with them the significant spiritual truths of heaven, hell, sin, and forgiveness. Love is a relational lubricant that allows us to speak boldly.

Lastly, be intentional to love those with riches. Who are the rich? One definition is: those who have extra beyond life's necessities. Or it could be someone who has more than you. Serve the wealthy without expecting anything in return, and you will earn the right to influence them for the Lord. Warn them to not let riches keep them from an intimate relationship with Jesus Christ. Help another avoid the place of torment by encouraging them to abandon themselves to Jesus.

"Command those who are rich in this present
world not to be arrogant nor to put their
hope in wealth, which is so uncertain, but to
put their hope in God" (1 Timothy 6:17).

Heavenly Father, I place my trust in Jesus Christ to save me from the place of torment.

Related Readings

Psalm 62:10; Jeremiah 49:4; Luke 12:20-21; John 5:24; 1 John 3:14

Faith Finds Jesus

*Since they could not get him to Jesus because of the crowd, they
made an opening in the roof above Jesus by digging through
it and then lowered the mat the man was lying on.*

MARK 2:4

Faith finds Jesus, especially when He seems hard to access. Faith is
persistent to get to God, because it knows He knows what's best.
Like a honeybee is drawn back to the honeycomb for community and
nutrition, so the soul is drawn to God by the Holy Spirit. In the presence of Jesus is forgiveness, healing, peace, and contentment. So, faith
does not rest until it rests in Christ. Forgiveness and healing, the fruits
of faith, depend upon faith and obedience. Faith finds Jesus.

Faith finds creative ways to bring friends and family to Jesus.
Because we enjoy the love, healing, and forgiveness of God, we want
others to have access to His life-changing blessings. We pray for opportunities to expose a person's felt need to the power of Christ's care. We
may invite them to a Christian concert to enjoy an uplifting night of
praise and worship. Or we can take them for coffee, listen to their hurts,
and pray for their heart to be healed by Jesus.

"The lord said unto the servant, Go out into the
highways and hedges, and compel them to come
in, that my house may be filled" (Luke 14:23 KJV).

Yes, our faith compels us to help friends find Jesus in personal salvation and forgiveness of sin. Perhaps we pick them up in our automobile, promise them lunch after church, and take them to hear the Bible taught and the gospel preached. Our part is to love people to the Lord, but it is God's part to change their heart. Faith finds Jesus.

Lastly, if our faith does not compel us to help others find faith, we may have a false faith, or at best an immature belief. Mature saints are moved to tears over the sin-stained souls of the lost. As we enjoy our sweet salvation, how can we sit still and not serve those who have yet to taste the satisfying grace of God? By God's grace we pray for innovative opportunities to bring people to Jesus. Perhaps we give a book, offer a prayer, share a video, or sit and listen. Faith finds Jesus!

"For Christ's love compels us, because we are convinced that one died for all…but for him who died for them and was raised again" (2 Corinthians 5:14-15).

Heavenly Father, I am so blessed to have found Jesus. Give me the faith and courage to help others find Christ.

Related Readings

Deuteronomy 4:29; Luke 7:48; Acts 5:39; Colossians 3:3

23

Christian Duty

You also, when you have done everything you were told to do, should
say, "We are unworthy servants; we have only done our duty."

LUKE 17:10

C hristian duty is illustrated by a master and servant relationship. The Master (Jesus Christ) is caring and clear in His expectations for His servants (Christians). The Master expects diligence and thoroughness in the tasks at hand. He does not patronize the sincere servant with flowery compliments, but allows the servant to enjoy fulfilling work for the Master's sake. Honorable service done for our Master Jesus Christ is the duty of all His followers. This is fundamental.

Our heavenly Father does not owe us anything for our routine or radical efforts for His kingdom. Indeed, our life in total is all grace. Our relationships, our ability to work, our mental reasoning, our feelings of love and hope all spring from the heart of our Savior Jesus. It is our duty to do what Christ commands without complaining or expecting anything in return. Like a good soldier does his duty for his country, so servants of Jesus are faithful to their charge.

⚬⚬⚬

"Fight the good fight of the faith. Take hold
of the eternal life to which you were called
when you made your good confession in the
presence of many witnesses" (1 Timothy 6:12).

Those of us who long for approval struggle when our service doesn't receive commendation. Yet this is a test: Are we motivated by what we might receive for obeying God, or do we serve simply to give to others and express our gratitude to Him? We become miserable, even angry, if we expect to be treated specially by the Lord or His people because of our sacrificial service. Yes, unexpected blessings will come back to those who bless, but this is not why we give. Our duty has no claims.

Therefore, your Christian duty is nothing more than to diligently follow Christ's calling. He is your Master and you serve at His bidding. He may have you engaged in the everyday tasks of motherhood or the basics of an entry-level job. Wherever the Lord has you on assignment, do it with joy. Total submission to Christ is your best option. Repent of negotiating for your own recognition and rewards. Christian duty, done by grace, glorifies God!

<hr />

"Fear God and keep his commandments, for this
is the duty of all mankind" (Ecclesiastes 12:13).

Heavenly Father, I submit to Your service and trust You to lead me in Your calling.

Related Readings
Job 22:2; Psalm 16:2; John 15:20; 1 Timothy 5:21

Unanswered Prayers

Then Jesus told his disciples a parable to show them
that they should always pray and not give up.

LUKE 18:1

Sometimes God is silent, even when His children cry out for answers. What doesn't seem fair becomes a test of faith that grows the prayer life of those who stay persistent with the Lord. No, He is not too busy answering the billion other prayers bombarding heaven, but He does want an unfeigned faith from His followers. God is not a "cosmic Google" waiting to give unlimited information to all requests. Too much data can break a spirit, puff up a mind, or confuse a heart.

Our heavenly Father knows what's best, though we wrestle with unanswered prayers. We may not be ready to receive what we want or think we need. We seem stuck in a stage of suffering because we are learning the depths of dependency on God. We feel like we are dog-paddling in a phase of waiting because our patience needs to progress to perseverance. Our aloneness can suffocate us, but we breathe better spiritually in a close walk with Christ. Unanswered prayers produce prayer.

"Be joyful in hope, patient in affliction,
faithful in prayer" (Romans 12:12).

Jesus says that even an unjust judge can be convinced of the right thing to do, but our heavenly Father does not have to be convinced of good actions. He is all good and He knows what's best for His children. He wants us to be convinced of the next right thing. So, a prolonged prayer process creates new convictions we cherish and cling to for comfort. For example, in prayer the Spirit may reveal anger in a pocket of our heart that He replaces with forgiveness. Unanswered prayer pushes us to unknown places that need soul care. Humble prayers are always productive.

Lastly, we remain in prayer to remain in Him. Our perspective grows in Christlike clairvoyance, as we focus on our heavenly Father in His liberal love and holiness. Trust, not suspicion, wins when we grow familiar with the dynamics of faithful living. Prayer becomes like oxygen for our soul, lest we smother ourselves in worry. Like a needy widow we need assurance from our righteous judge, Jesus! Yes, our Lord never sleeps; He listens intently and loves us passionately.

—⁂—

"While he was speaking to me, I was
in a deep sleep" (Daniel 8:18).

Heavenly Father, while I wait on You, I will pray to You and remain in You.

Related Readings
Isaiah 40:31; Luke 11:5-8; Romans 1:9-10; Ephesians 6:18;
    Colossians 4:2

25

Unacceptable Prayers

❧

*To some who were confident of their own righteousness and looked
down on everyone else, Jesus told this parable… "The Pharisee stood by
himself and prayed: 'God, I thank you that I am not like other people.'"*

LUKE 18:9,11

Unacceptable prayers come from a proud heart. The self-righteous
look down on others different from themselves and find pleasure in publicly praying about their moral inferiority. Yes, those who
use their prayers to "preach" at others are conceited in their own high-
mindedness. Prayer is not meant to flaunt a person's faith, but to model
the need for mercy from the Almighty! Proud prayers focus on mankind, not on mankind's Maker. However, humility qualifies quality
prayers.

We first prepare our hearts with humble submission to Almighty
God. Our heavenly Father looks for humility as an indicator of good
and acceptable prayers. Time constraints push us to transactional
prayers, while our Lord and Savior Jesus longs for relational prayers.
Humble prayers engage in conversation with Christ, listening most of
the time, if not the entire time. Our patient prayers enable us to remain
in the presence of Jesus until we get to know Him.

❧

"All of us have become like one who is unclean,
and all our righteous acts are like filthy rags;
we all shrivel up like a leaf,
and like the wind our sins sweep us away" (Isaiah 64:6).

The Righteous One reminds us that our righteous acts outside of
Christ are like filthy rags. Only to the cross do we cling, as we bring

ourselves into the presence of Holy God. He is the object of our worship. He is whom we bow to in awe and adoration. He is whom we cry out to for mercy, grace, and forgiveness. He is whom we petition in our pain. He is the One with whom we sit silently in sweet surrender and trust. He loves and comforts us, so we can love and comfort others.

You may feel distant from God in your sorrow, but He invites you to come closer and feel His comforting presence. Moreover, sin doesn't disqualify you from prayer—it qualifies you. It's out of your weakness that He makes you strong. It is out of your despair that He repairs your mind, will, and emotions. Bring your successes and failures to the feet of Jesus as an offering of praise. He takes what is dedicated to Him and multiplies it for His glory. Humility prays acceptable prayers!

———

"You also, like living stones, are being built
into a spiritual house to be a holy priesthood,
offering spiritual sacrifices acceptable to
God through Jesus Christ" (1 Peter 2:5).

Heavenly Father, may my prayers be humble and acceptable to You.

Related Readings
Psalm 18:27; Isaiah 66:2; Jeremiah 31:19; Luke 1:52; 1 Timothy 1:15

26

Work in Retirement

―――――― ∞◎∞ ――――――

At five o'clock he went back and found still others standing around. He said, "Why are you standing around all day doing nothing?" They said, "Because no one hired us." He told them to go to work in his vineyard.

\text{MATTHEW 20:5-7 MSG}

The spiritual age of retirement is not the same as the secular age of retirement. Retirement from God's work comes after death, not in this life. Followers of Jesus are not idle, caught up in their own issues; rather, they look for ways to work for the Lord. Maybe they greet people with a smile at church, sing in the choir, serve on the board, teach preschoolers, or manage the ministry's finances. Freedom from the shackles of secular work is to serve others, not to pamper self.

Culture claims that those over age 65 live for themselves in travel, ease, and pleasure. It's all about indulging the flesh and starving the spirit, or perhaps tipping a charity or two. But our Lord Jesus calls us to remain engaged in His eternal agenda: evangelism, discipleship, mentoring, and giving our time, talents, and treasures. The gospel of Jesus Christ allows an old soul to remain young at heart. You truly learn to live when you lean into the Lord in your golden years!

――――― ∞◎∞ ―――――

> "They will still bear fruit in old age,
> they will stay fresh and green,
> proclaiming, 'The LORD is upright;
> he is my Rock'" (Psalm 92:14-15).

Are you in the empty-nest season with an available schedule? Perhaps you host young couples in your home for a meal and Bible study. Are you doing life with those you can invest in and with those who can invest in you? If your soul idles long enough in isolation it will dry up and die. However, as you engage your energy in others, you will come alive for another day. Perhaps you adopt or foster children, or invite your parents, who selflessly cared for you, to live with you.

Lastly, keep the vineyard of your heart and mind free from the kudzu of lazy living and empty thinking. Aggressively pray for your children and grandchildren to fall deeper in love with Jesus and with each other. Daily move your body outside into the Lord's creation. Push through deadly inertia with a lively walk. Fresh air clears your mind and lifts your gaze upward to God. Let the sun warm your face with the caresses of your Father's Son. Work for the Lord until the day comes when you go to be with the Lord. He rewards those who work for Him!

"That person is like a tree planted by streams of water,
which yields its fruit in season
and whose leaf does not wither—
whatever they do prospers" (Psalm 1:3).

Heavenly Father, may my work for You not cease, and may it be pleasing to You.

Related Readings

Proverbs 11:30; Ecclesiastes 7:10; Romans 9:12; 1 Timothy 5:1-2;
    Titus 2:2

27

The Prayer of Jesus

*One day Jesus was praying in a certain place. When he finished,
one of his disciples said to him, "Lord, teach us to pray, just as
John taught his disciples." He said to them, "When you pray,
say: Father, hallowed be your name, your kingdom come."*

LUKE 11:1-2

The prayer of Jesus, otherwise known as the Lord's Prayer, is our model for prayer. Jesus, in customary fashion, created consistent time to be with His heavenly Father. One day, upon conclusion of His private prayers, a perceptive disciple asked Jesus for prayer instruction for himself and the other disciples. Yes, this prayer of Jesus's was birthed out of intimacy with His heavenly Father. He instructed on prayer with authority because He prayed with authority.

The prayer of Jesus is as much about the spirit of the prayer as it is the words of the prayer. Indeed, the Lord spoke about prayer having just prayed. Only minutes before He had bowed in humble worship seeking the face of His heavenly Father. He gloried in the glory of the One from heaven who sent Him to earth to save the world. Oh, what a privilege to pray in the presence of our wisdom-filled God. Our spirits are expunged of all selfish pride and replenished with selfless humility. The reverent and submissive spirit of our Lord's prayer is the navigator for our prayers.

"The spirit is willing, but the flesh
is weak" (Matthew 26:41).

Our flesh seeks to dismiss the power of prayer by questioning its effectiveness. "Does it really matter whether I pray?" "Are things truly any different after I pray than before I pray?" In His prayer Jesus desires all men and women everywhere to pray with hands lifted high in praise and hearts bowed low in protracted submission. He's heavenly minded with earthly aspirations. He prays for God's kingdom to be ushered onto earth with the splendor of heaven's resources. Our globe governed by God, for God and with God. The prayer of Jesus pronounces God king!

Furthermore, the prayer of Jesus is our model of how and what to pray. Begin and end with Him. Satan shrinks back at the supplicants set forth by our Savior. Thus, we take to heart the heart of our Lord in His instructions to pray. The words are not a magical chant, but rather a divine mandate to seek the love of our heavenly Father, fear His holiness, align with His will, ask His provision, receive His forgiveness, trust His power, and announce His glory. Pray His prayer as your prayer!

"I will certainly pray to the Lord your God as
you have requested" (Jeremiah 42:4).

Heavenly Father, my prayer is that the prayer of Jesus be my pattern for prayer.

Related Readings
1 Chronicles 29:10; Daniel 9:3-4; Acts 4:24; 2 Thessalonians 1:12

28

Instant Obedience

❧

There was a man who had two sons. He went to the first
and said, "Son, go and work today in the vineyard." "I
will not," he answered, but later he changed his mind and
went. Then the father went to the other son and said the
same thing. He answered, "I will, sir," but he did not go.

MATTHEW 21:28-30

Instant obedience is an indicator of a heart that loves God. Someone who first says no to the Lord, but later repents and obeys, enjoys His mercy. However, someone who immediately says yes but never follows through is a liar who misses God's mercy. Yes, an oath of obedience to Jesus Christ is a promise requiring swift action. An honest answer of no to the Almighty can be converted to obedience, but a dishonest yes that passively disobeys is absent of moral authority.

Do you sometimes catch yourself agreeing just to appease an authority, with no intention of following through? Or do you measure your words and commitments with a genuine goal to get it done? Appeasement to gain harmony in the short term will only compound disappointment in the long term. It is better to be up front and experience some disapproval than to mask your true intentions until they are revealed in a dramatic disclosure. Obedience begins with transparency.

❧

"For I say to you, that unless your righteousness
exceeds the righteousness of the scribes and
Pharisees, you will by no means enter the
kingdom of heaven" (Matthew 5:20 NKJV).

Those who hide behind religious activity with no intentions of authentic obedience to God will miss His blessings, even salvation. The kingdom of heaven is not made with hands, but is birthed in hearts that repent and believe the gospel of Jesus Christ. We who brand ourselves Christians have to honestly ask, which kingdom are we building, His or ours? When we turn over control to Christ, we can rest in Him. We trust and obey for this is the gate to God's will.

Where is your heavenly Father calling you to obey Him? Perhaps there is a relationship that needs to cease, a job that needs to change, or a friend you need to forgive. Christ may be calling you overseas for a season or to a city closer to your family. Whatever and wherever the Holy Spirit is prompting your heart, don't delay; rather, instantly obey the Spirit's leading. You may have said no, only to realize your mistake. Change your mind, swallow your pride, and obey!

"Before I was afflicted I went astray,
but now I obey your word" (Psalm 119:67).

Heavenly Father, give me the wisdom to know what to do and the courage to do it.

Related Readings

Jonah 3:3; John 8:51; Romans 6:17; Philippians 2:12; 1 Peter 1:22

29

Rejection to Restoration

The stone the builders rejected has become the cornerstone;
the Lord has done this, and it is marvelous in our eyes.

MARK 12:10-11

What is rejected can be restored by God. People can reject a good person, even a godly person, only to see themselves discredited and their object of contempt reinstated. The majority may miss the right conclusion, because the facts were withheld by a jealous few. Thus, beware of someone or a group with persuasive powers and shady motives. Make sure all the facts have been flushed out before choosing sides. Those whose power is threatened will threaten their foes.

Jesus was rejected by the religious elite only to be resurrected as Lord by His heavenly Father. A few, green with envy, branded Jesus and His followers as power hungry political fanatics. However, heaven did not sit still in the face of these false accusations. The One whose character was assassinated and whose body was crucified became the payment for His critics' sin. We can reject Jesus as our Savior, but belief in Him is still required for a right relationship with God.

"So this is what the Sovereign LORD says:
'See, I lay a stone in Zion, a tested stone,
a precious cornerstone for a sure foundation;
the one who relies on it
will never be stricken with panic'" (Isaiah 28:16).

When we accept Christ, He brings us back to God. Our arrogant intellect rejected the existence of a personal God, but since He restored us to Himself we crave His company. Our self-reliant spirit dismissed dependency on the Almighty, but now we are strengthened in Him. Our drive to accomplish ignored His grace, but now having tasted God's grace, we hunger for more. Our pride looked down on spiritual people, but now our humility compels us to look up to heaven for help!

Therefore, be a restorer of relationships, not a rejecter. Who needs your intentional investment of time so they can be brought back into your good graces? You are the Lord's minister of reconciliation. Because Christ is the capstone of your character, you have the honor of laying His cornerstone of convictions in the lives of your children and grand-children. Invite those who have rejected Jesus to accept Him. Like a refurbished piece of furniture, His restoration is beautiful!

—⌘—

"If you return to the Almighty, you
will be restored" (Job 22:23).

Heavenly Father, thank You for receiving me into Your family of faith.

Related Readings

Job 42:10; Psalm 51:12; Ephesians 2:20; 1 Peter 2:7

30

Comfort in Loss

——⦿——

*Many Jews had come to Martha and Mary to
comfort them in the loss of their brother.*

JOHN 11:19

Have you lost someone or something close to your heart—a baby, a spouse, a friend, a job, or an opportunity? A great loss requires great grace or the pain is unbearable. Why do some expectant mothers have a stillborn child and others don't? Can we truly understand these puzzling matters until we get to heaven and are able to ask, "Why, Lord, why?"

Where is God when emotions run raw and a great hole of hurt embeds the heart? We don't always understand the ways of God, but we can always count on Christ's comfort. The Lord lingers long with those caught in the pain of great loss. What others cannot totally understand, your heavenly Father fully comprehends. Grace soothes aching hearts. Christ's comfort nurses like cool cough syrup flowing down a swollen, inflamed throat.

——⦿——

"For just as we share abundantly in the sufferings
of Christ, so also our comfort abounds
through Christ" (2 Corinthians 1:5).

The Lord's comfort is limitless in its capacity to cure.

Furthermore, Christ comforts us, so we are able to extend His compelling comfort to others. Productive pain pays it forward in a faith-based solution to other sad souls. Giving is therapy in God's economy, so those of us saved by grace are not stingy with its application. Who do you know that needs a listening ear, a silent prayer, or a caring visit?

If comfort is kept closed up in the closet of our busyness, then we miss out on one of life's great joys. Shame on any servant of Jesus that only has time to hear the heart of the spiritually healthy. Be aware as tears pool under the surface of a tender heart in your circle of influence. Look around. Who is struggling with health, work, or relational issues? Comfort them, as your influence ripples like a rock slicing through a still body of water.

Say a prayer for someone in despair, send flowers to a young mom who just lost her little one after the first trimester of pregnancy, network for an acquaintance in career transition, pay the rent for a struggling relative, or introduce someone broken to the uplifting love and saving power of Jesus Christ. Comfort is your platform to proclaim God's grace.

———

"Praise be to the God and Father of our Lord Jesus
Christ, the Father of compassion and the God of
all comfort, who comforts us in all our troubles,
so that we can comfort" (2 Corinthians 1:3-4).

Where do I need Christ's comfort and who do I know that needs His comfort and joy?

Related Readings

Job 42:11; Psalms 86:17; 119:76; John 14:1; 2 Corinthians 7:6-7

31

Come and See

‐‐‐‐‐‐ ᢙᢚ ‐‐‐‐‐‐

Philip found Nathanael and told him, "We have found the one Moses
wrote about in the Law, and about whom the prophets also wrote—
Jesus of Nazareth, the son of Joseph."
"Nazareth! Can anything good come from there?" Nathanael asked.
"Come and see," said Philip.

JOHN 1:45-46

Come and see. Come and see Jesus the Son of God. Come and see Jesus the Savior of the world. Come and see Jesus the forgiver of sins. Come and see Jesus, a best friend and servant. Come and see Jesus: teacher, student, and healer. Come and see Jesus: Master, Lord, and King of kings. Come and see Jesus and be saved forevermore. Eyes of faith feast on a relationship with Jesus.

We have the privilege as Christ followers to invite people to come and see Jesus. When the lost encounter Christ they can see the way more clearly. By God's grace, seekers can see His work of grace in our speech and in our unspoken words. They see our kindness in the face of unkindness. They see our respect when we are disrespected. They see our love when we are unloved. They see us forgive when we are rejected. Christ in us is a window into the wonders of God's grace.

‐‐‐‐‐‐ ᢙᢚ ‐‐‐‐‐‐

"You show that you are a letter from Christ, the result
of our ministry, written not with ink but with the
Spirit of the living God, not on tablets of stone but
on tablets of human hearts" (2 Corinthians 3:3).

Who do you know who needs to know God? Who can you invite to come and see Jesus? Indeed, you earn the right to invite by first investing in their life. You invest, then you invite. You invest in prayer and fasting for a friend to come to faith. You invest in caring for a child, so perhaps their parents might become children of God. You invest financially in a needy family, so they can receive the true riches of a relationship and fellowship with Christ.

You appeal to a person's intellect with Christ's fulfillment of prophecy, and then conversion to Him is sealed when they experience Jesus in their heart. Facts without faith create knowledge unredeemed. But when you introduce others to Jesus in a loving relationship, they are redeemed by Jesus. Keep your passionate fellowship with your Savior fresh and you will naturally want others to meet your best friend. You can say, "Come and see Jesus," because you have seen Jesus!

―――∞∞――

"You will be his witness to all people of what
you have seen and heard" (Acts 22:15).

Heavenly Father, give me courage to invite others to come and see Christ.

Related Readings
Job 13:1; Isaiah 66:19; 1 Corinthians 2:9; 1 John 1:1

32

Who Is Jesus?

⚬⚬⚬

"But what about you?" he asked. "Who do you say I am?"
Simon Peter answered, "You are the
Messiah, the Son of the living God."

MATTHEW 16:15-16

There will always be those who deny the deity of Christ. They try to dilute His status as Savior by calling Him a healer—like a medical practitioner of today, but without supernatural intercession. Other skeptics seek to corral Christ into a group of good moral teachers who had good things to say, but they certainly do not recognize Him as the Son of God.

However, God reveals to those who believe that the Son of man was also the Son of God. John the Baptist was humble and bold, but only a man. Elijah was a prophet called by the Lord, but a man nonetheless. Jeremiah was full of passion and love for his people, but he was a man and not the Messiah Christ, who was to come. Jesus is the Son of the living God. When asked if He was the One, Jesus did not stutter. He offered evidence for this fact.

> The Jews who were there gathered around him, saying, "How long will you keep us in suspense? If you are the Messiah, tell us plainly."
> Jesus answered, "I did tell you, but you do not believe. The works I do in my Father's name testify about me" (John 10:24-25).

Faith is the first step to accepting Jesus Christ as the Son of God, who died on the cross for your sins and rose from the dead to give you life eternal. Because you base your belief on the historical knowledge of

Christ's claim to be God, you are in good company with thousands of His contemporaries, who also believed based on His words and deeds. Facts become understanding when you apply faith and trust in Jesus.

When you walk closely with Christ, you confess with conviction that He is the Son of the living God. You are blessed when you are bold in your belief, because you bolster the faith of others in Jesus. Don't be shy about your Savior when people ask, "Who is Jesus?" Tell them that He is the way to God, the truth of God, and the life of God.

———∞∞———

"Jesus answered, 'I am the way and the truth
and the life. No one comes to the Father
except through me'" (John 14:6).

Can Christ count on me to give a clear account of who He is and what He expects?

Related Readings

Isaiah 53:1-12; Jeremiah 10:10; John 1:29; Hebrews 3:12-13

33

Concerns of God

When Jesus turned and looked at his disciples, he rebuked Peter. "Get behind me, Satan!" he said. "You do not have in mind the concerns of God, but merely human concerns."

MARK 8:33

What concerns God? What does the Almighty deem as the most important? The Lord is concerned that His will be done on earth as it is in heaven. He accepts those who submit their will to His, but He rejects those who impose their will onto His. God is concerned with building His kingdom, not man's kingdom. The kingdom of heaven begins in our hearts with love and obedience to King Jesus. A citizen of Christ's country is concerned about promoting His fame.

Moreover, our heavenly Father is concerned with keeping His promises to His people. For example, He shows up in answered prayer to assure us that we are not alone. He is concerned for us when we fear giving a public speech. Not only does He give us insight and clarity in our preparation, but He also prepares the hearts of the people who hear our talk. He blesses our words of instruction and inspiration. He wants us to feel His peace, as we present His timeless principles.

"God heard their groaning and he remembered his covenant with Abraham, with Isaac and with Jacob. So God looked on the Israelites and was concerned about them" (Exodus 2:24-25).

Your heavenly Father is also concerned about your suffering. His heart goes out to you when your heart has been broken. The Lord longs for wholeness in your body, soul, and spirit. If you are detached from your true feelings, He wants to reengage you with your emotions. He wants you in touch with your feelings, so you can feel the needs of others. Your Savior Jesus meets you in your place of suffering with His sensitive comfort. He empathizes with your cry for His care.

Furthermore, you partner with the Holy Spirit when you keep the concerns of God in the forefront of your mind. Yes, keep Christ's concerns your priority and your human concerns will not keep you from Christ. Jesus bluntly brands self-seeking distractors as agents of the enemy. Beware of people who talk spiritual talk but are more concerned about their own agenda than God's. Concern yourself with His concerns, and your human concerns will fade away. Be concerned where He's concerned!

"The LORD said, 'I have indeed seen the misery of my people in Egypt. I have heard them crying out because of their slave drivers, and I am concerned about their suffering'" (Exodus 3:7).

Heavenly Father, keep my concerns in line with Your concerns.

Related Readings

Exodus 4:31; Luke 1:25; Acts 7:31-32; 1 Corinthians 7:32; 2 Thessalonians 2:1-3

34

Truth of Lies

⸺⟪∞⟫⸺

Jesus answered, "I am the way and the truth and the life."

JOHN 14:6

When [the devil] lies, he speaks his native language,
for he is a liar and the father of lies.

JOHN 8:44

Truth flows from the One who is the Truth—Jesus. Lies flow from the father of lies—the devil. So, truth tellers side with the Lord and liars side with Satan. With whom do we align? We are quick to say Jesus, but in everyday life, if not careful, we drift into representing the dark side when tempted to speak untruth out of fear, instead of truth out of trust.

Lying is so short-term focused. We are afraid we will lose something if we don't lie. We may lose someone's respect, but when we are found out to be a liar, it is compounded into humiliation. We may lose money, but when indiscretions are exposed over time, we lose more in compromised credibility. Better to lose a little with honesty than a lot with lies.

⸺⟪∞⟫⸺

"If we claim to have fellowship with him
and yet walk in the darkness, we lie and
do not live out the truth" (1 John 1:6).

In paradise, the first lie was presented by the serpent as he led Eve to believe she could be like God. Some things never change. Every day we are tempted to promote ourselves as someone better than our real self. But instead, Spirit-led living looks to exalt Christ and others, not self. To be honest is to take responsibility for our actions, not to blame.

———∞∞∞———

"The man said, 'The woman you put here with me—
she gave me some fruit from the tree, and I ate
it.' Then the LORD God said to the woman, 'What is
this you have done?' The woman said, 'The serpent
deceived me, and I ate'" (Genesis 3:12-13).

Are you honest with yourself about constant exposure to a compromising situation? Are you loose with the truth, or do you speak directly and include all the information? Take responsibility for wrong decisions and going forward seek sound advice from friends who will tell you the truth. Be totally honest with them so they can offer the best advice. Begin by coming clean with Christ. He already knows, so be totally open and real with others.

———∞∞∞———

"Friend deceives friend, and no one speaks the
truth. They have taught their tongues to lie; they
weary themselves with sinning" (Jeremiah 9:5).

What do I need to be honest about with God and myself? Who needs my complete honesty?

Related Readings
Proverbs 12:17; Jeremiah 9:3; Romans 1:25; 1 John 2:21

35

Hearing and Listening

─────⊙⊙⊙─────

Then they asked him, "What did [Jesus] do to you?
How did he open your eyes?"
He answered, "I have told you already and you did not listen.
Why do you want to hear it again? Do you
want to become his disciples too?"

JOHN 9:26-27

Hearing does not guarantee listening. Eye contact and engaged body language can still lead to no heart comprehension. Someone can act like they are listening without really understanding. People who lack humility and empathy lack the ability to really listen well. Pride and ego run over another's sentences before they finish. An unbridled intellect interrupts with solutions and new ideas before they truly listen to the heart of the one making conversation. Hubris is deaf.

So, there is skill involved in learning to listen with understanding. Good listeners lean into the one speaking and seek to know what the one speaking knows. They take in the spoken words and simultaneously process the emotional meaning behind the speech. Listeners hear without any preconceived notions or preemptive conclusions. We hear and listen well when we enter into the emotional world of the speaker. We learn to listen by asking clarifying questions.

─────⊙⊙⊙─────

"After three days they found [Jesus] in the temple
courts, sitting among the teachers, listening to
them and asking them questions" (Luke 2:46).

The Holy Spirit is also involved in illuminating true meaning and providing discernment to humble and wise hearts. So, we prayerfully listen beyond the logic of the spoken language to the unspoken prompt-ings of God's Spirit. A person's words may say they want one thing, but in their heart of hearts, they know they need something different. The Lord's Spirit working through your spirit will give you insight into what they need to consider. Listen for the Spirit's quiet leading.

Most of all, be a hearer, listener, and a doer of God's Word. Scrip-ture is like fertilizer for your faith. If the Bible is only revered on a book-shelf, it is useless; but if it is spread over your life, it makes things grow. Therefore, hear, listen, and apply God's Holy Word to your life. Once you listen and learn, allow His truth to transform your being. Wise listeners of Christ's words integrate His principles into their behavior. They pray, "Speak, Lord, for I am listening for You."

"Speak, LORD, for your servant is
listening" (1 Samuel 3:9).

Heavenly Father, speak to my heart. I will truly listen to You and obey.

Related Readings

Deuteronomy 34:9; Job 38:1-3; 1 Corinthians 14:21; Hebrews 4:12;
    1 John 4:6

36

Result of Worry

Can any one of you by worrying add a single hour to your life?

MATTHEW 6:27

The results of worry aren't redeeming, productive, or helpful. Worry doesn't assist today, and it only complicates tomorrow. Its sideways energy sidetracks us from our heavenly Father's loving comfort. Worry is a dark alley in a loud, confused city. It's an untrodden trail off the beaten path of God's will. Worry has a way of putting a wrench into the works of Christ. It's a subtle and not so subtle way to place our own efforts ahead of God's. Worry leads to a victim mindset.

Worry can become a self-fulfilling prophecy. Yes, we can work ourselves into a frantic state of self-reliance, so much so that we begin to believe and live out lies. We predict the worst-case scenario is imminent, and then we act in ways that move us in that direction. We simmer in self-pity, talking like a victim, then we become a victim. Worry whispers statements like, "What if you lose your job? What if you have a disease? What if your partner leaves you?" Worry's results wreak havoc.

"Let the peace of Christ rule in your hearts, since as members of one body you were called to peace. And be thankful" (Colossians 3:15).

Praise the Lord there are remedies to worry! Shifting our focus from self to our Savior is a foolproof way to preempt false thinking with faith. Self is like a jealous lover who wants to be the center of attention, but Christ alone deserves this highest status of affection. When our idols of security, money, control, and comfort bow to Jesus, worry runs away rejected. Worship embraces hope as courage for the heart. Courage and hope are fraternal twins that birth in us a living faith.

Furthermore, the Lord sustains you when you cast your cares on Him. Your humility in confessing your ongoing need for Christ leads to spiritual sustainability. Staying spiritually healthy requires you to invite your heavenly Father to care for your anxious heart and nervous emotions. Submission to Sovereign God precludes a position for your pride to perch. Yes, Jesus's spoken word in Scripture soothes your soul and brings peace to your war of worry. The result of trust is peace and calm.

<hr />

"Humble yourselves, therefore, under God's mighty hand, that he may lift you up in due time. Cast all your anxiety on him because he cares for you" (1 Peter 5:6-7).

Heavenly Father, I bow in humility to You, trusting You with my cares and concerns.

Related Readings

Psalm 55:22; Proverbs 12:25; Philippians 4:6-7; Hebrews 13:5-6

37

Follow Jesus First

When Jesus saw the crowd around him, he gave orders to cross to the other side of the lake. Then a teacher of the law came to him and said, "Teacher, I will follow you wherever you go."

MATTHEW 8:18-19

Good leaders are first good followers. Do you follow the orders of Jesus? When He asks you to do something uncomfortable, do you move out of your comfort zone with confidence? Compelling Christian leadership has focused "followship" on their Master, the Lord Jesus. Where is He asking you to go that requires sacrifice and unconditional commitment? His orders do not always make sense, but they are totally trustworthy and helpful.

When He directs you to leave the noise of the crowds for the quietness of a few, do not delay. If you are obsessed by activity, you can easily lose your edge on energy and faith. When all my oomph is consumed by serving every request and answering every call, I have no time or concentration to hear from Christ. What is He saying? This is the most important inquiry I can make. What is Jesus telling me to do? So, when I listen, I learn.

You may be in the middle of a monster season of success, so make sure your achievements do not muffle the Lord's message. It's when we are fast and furious that our faith becomes perfunctory and predictable. Leadership requires time alone to retool and recalibrate our character. People follow when they know you've been with Jesus.

The most difficult part may be the transition from doing less, to listening and thinking more. If you, as the leader, are not planning ahead, who is? Who has the best interests of the enterprise in mind? Who is defending the mission and vision of the organization, so there is not a drift into competing strategies? Follow Jesus first—then He frees you to see.

Where is the Lord leading you to go? Will you lag behind with excellent excuses, or will you make haste and move forward by faith? Go with God and He will direct you through the storms of change. He may seem silent at times, but remember: He led you to this place, and where He leads, He provides. Follow Jesus first, then go wherever He goes. You will lose people in the process, but you will gain better people for His next phase.

∽∽∽

> "Then Jesus said to his disciples, 'Whoever wants to be my disciple must deny themselves and take up their cross and follow me'" (Matthew 16:24).

Where is Jesus leading me to go? Am I willing to let go and trust Him with what's next?

Related Readings

Numbers 32:11; Isaiah 8:10-12; 1 Corinthians 1:11-13; Revelation 14:4

38

Unholy Accolades

*Woe to you when everyone speaks well of you, for that
is how their ancestors treated the false prophets.*

LUKE 6:26

Authentic teachers and preachers of the Bible will have some who disagree with, even dismiss their proclamations of truth. If a spokesperson for the Lord is not criticized by some, they may be watering down God's Word. Churches are not created to make everyone feel good, but to lead them to faith in Christ and holy living.

Furthermore, it is important how the messenger delivers the message—not with a holier-than-thou disposition, but in a spirit of compassion and humble boldness. Followers of Jesus are not out to intentionally offend and attack those who embrace untruth or a worldly way of living. Instead, we are to speak the truth in love and trust God with how people will respond. Do not be shy about your convictions, but share with godly grace.

Has a vocal minority unfairly criticized your stand on marriage? Do some of your family members think you are strange because of the way you raise your children in Christ? Have some at work labeled you as a narrow-minded Christian? If so, do not be ashamed that some do not speak well of you. Sometimes we are best known by our enemies.

"Do not be ashamed of the testimony about our Lord
or of me his prisoner. Rather, join with me in suffering
for the gospel, by the power of God" (2 Timothy 1:8).

Enemies of the cross are enemies of those who daily bear their cross for Christ's sake. But we engage the enemy in prayer and through spiritual warfare. The war is not won in the headline of a newspaper or in a debate on national television; the war is won as followers of Jesus flood heaven with faithful petitions and engage people with loving truth. The goal is not to win an agreement, but to live a life worthy of the gospel.

Have you compromised the Lord's standards because of pressure from someone you want to please? If so, dismiss the praise and applause of people and seek accolades from Almighty God. It is easy to stand on principle when everyone is happy, but the true test of your convictions in Christ come when people are not happy with your righteous acts. An attractive life full of Christ's character is countercultural, but it points people to Him.

⸺⸺∞⸺⸺

> "For, as I have often told you before and now tell you again even with tears, many live as enemies of the cross of Christ" (Philippians 3:18).

Am I too timid to tell the truth? How can I turn my shyness about Jesus into a bold display?

Related Readings

2 Chronicles 6:34-35; Jeremiah 14:14; Matthew 7:15; 1 Peter 4:2-4

39

Consumer Christianity

꧰

*Then he said to them all: "Whoever wants to be my disciple must
deny themselves and take up their cross daily and follow me."*

LUKE 9:23

onsumer Christianity is about me—what I receive from my experience with God, what I gain in the worship service, what I learn
from the pastor's sermon, how I will be blessed because I attended
church. Consumer Christianity is a receiving mentality, not a giving
one. If I am not intentional, I can drift into a totally selfish scenario
regarding my expectations in my spiritual life. I place my needs above
the needs of everyone else, and I leverage my relationship with the
Lord for myself.

However, Jesus describes His followers as cross carriers, not con-
sumers. He said the role of His disciple is death to self and life for Him.
Christ meets the needs of cross bearers. For example, in the process of
pointing others to Jesus our need for significance is met. We worship
Him in the glory of His grandeur and experience peace. Cross-carrying
Christianity means that the Holy Spirit applies what we learn in Bible
study to our hearts. His truth transforms us into His likeness.

꧰

"Offer your bodies as a living sacrifice, holy and
pleasing to God—this is your true and proper
worship. Do not conform to the pattern of this
world, but be transformed by the renewing of
your mind. Then you will be able to test and
approve what God's will is" (Romans 12:1-2).

Churches need to guard against creating a culture of consumer

Christianity. Relationship with Christ is a covenant. Salvation is free, but discipleship is costly. Our trust in Jesus requires our letting go of our trust in anything else. Our confession and contrition over sin longs to grow in the grace and holiness of the Lord Jesus Christ. Our repentance turns from old, selfish thinking and replaces it with new, selfless thinking. Cross-carrying churches create cross-carrying Christians.

Furthermore, our ability to follow Christ is sustained by grace through faith. Grace governs the heart in humility. Faith feeds the mind with hope. We follow hard after Jesus when we have been with Jesus. In our intimate moments of prayer, the Holy Spirit gives us the spiritual energy to engage the world with truth and grace. Therefore, be a cross-carrying Christian who challenges consumer Christians to engage in discipleship. Self-denial frees us to follow Jesus!

―――∽∞∾―――

"Live as free people, but do not use your freedom as a cover-up for evil; live as God's slaves" (1 Peter 2:16).

Heavenly Father, create in me a cross-carrying heart and not a consumer Christian heart.

Related Readings
Leviticus 16:31; Philippians 1:21; Galatians 5:13; Hebrews 9:15

40

Make Things Right

Settle matters quickly with your adversary who is taking you to court.

MATTHEW 5:25

Make things right with those you have wronged or who have wronged you. If you stay engaged in a stalemate of accusations, you may end up in court. Why involve civil authorities when Christ has given you a game plan for reconciliation? By faith, call an accusatory cease-fire with your adversary. Take the first step to reach out and request a meeting or phone call. Better to get together with cool heads than to stay mad separately. Don't allow matters to escalate to a heated crisis.

Humbly agree with your adversary. If they feel hurt by you, apologize for hurting their heart. If they feel misunderstood by you, say "I'm sorry" and listen intently to what they are trying to convey. If they feel heard by you, you may not have to say a word. When you listen well you communicate love, respect, and patience. Validate your accuser's feelings and you validate them. Take responsibility for your actions and seek to be reconciled to your adversary.

∞∞

"If you are offering your gift at the altar and there remember that your brother or sister has something against you, leave your gift there in front of the altar. First go and be reconciled to them; then come and offer your gift" (Matthew 5:23-24).

Furthermore, a fractured relationship with someone on earth hinders our relationship with God in heaven. We cannot stay focused by faith on our heavenly Father when we have broken the trust of another brother or sister. Our conscience will not be clear before Christ if it is not clear before the one we've offended. Yes, taking the time to build a bridge of acceptance over a chasm of rejection is evidence that God has reconciled us to Himself through His Son Jesus Christ.

Sometimes when we soften our hearts, their heart softens too. As we calm the tone of our words and lower the volume of our voice, our accusers might do the same. As we take a step toward them, they may take a step toward us. Therefore, don't wait on your adversary to make the first move. Make things right by deciding not to fight. Go humble yourself and agree with them, and you both will win. Make things right on earth so you are qualified to make things right with God in heaven.

"Whoever claims to love God yet hates a brother or sister is a liar. For whoever does not love their brother and sister, whom they have seen, cannot love God, whom they have not seen" (1 John 4:20).

Heavenly Father, give me the humility and courage to listen to the one I've offended.

Related Readings

Proverbs 6:1-5; 2 Corinthians 5:20; 1 John 4:12

41

Kind but Direct

~~~~~~

Let your "Yes" be "Yes," and your "No," "No."
MATTHEW 5:37 NKJV

Love uses direct language laced in grace. There is no ambiguity with those who care about communicating clearly from a caring heart. Yes, they risk hurting someone's feelings by being forthcoming with the facts, but better for the hearer to be aware and adjust now than to remain ignorant and unmoved. Insightful questions from a compassionate heart are a respectful way to show someone the way. Indeed, kind but direct conversations grow deeper relationships.

Yes, wise are we to receive what may feel like a rough response from a friend. Because they love us, they will not leave us to languish in unwise behavior. When we are blinded by our own ambition, greed, or self-righteousness, we need words from our spouse, boss, or mentor that challenge our unhealthy thinking. Our ability, by God's grace, to ingest another's instruction into our mind and heart moves us closer to Christ. Be grateful for good friends who don't hold back.

~~~~~~

"Anxiety weighs down the heart,
but a kind word cheers it up" (Proverbs 12:25).

Therefore, pray and prepare your heart before you deliver a direct message to one who means so much to you and to your Master Jesus. See them as the Lord sees them: a sheep without a shepherd, a child in need of nurture, or a novice hiker in want of a guide. Take the time to tell a loved one the truth in love, and one day they may thank you. Better for them to be a little offended now than to wander down a destructive path later. Love is kind but direct.

Moreover, make sure to cultivate a culture of prayer in your home and community of friends. Prayer is relational lubricant that opens the heart of those who need to hear. It gives grace and courage to those whose speech needs to be straightforward. Talk with the Lord before you talk with those who need the Lord. Better to have a little talk with Jesus before you have a big talk with a child or coworker. Your initiative to kindly instruct another in God's ways is a gift.

⸺⸻⸺

"The wise in heart are called discerning,
and gracious words promote
instruction" (Proverbs 16:21).

Heavenly Father, use me to speak kindly to those who need a gracious but direct word.

Related Readings

Proverbs 8:33; 9:9; Jeremiah 17:7; Acts 5:40; 1 Corinthians 1:5; Titus 2:8

42

Poor Jesus

⸺◦∞◦⸺

You know the grace of our Lord Jesus Christ, that though
he was rich, yet for your sake he became poor, so that
you through his poverty might become rich.

2 Corinthians 8:9

Jesus was poor. He owned nothing but had everything He needed. He borrowed boats, donkeys, food, and lodging. He lived on borrowed time—then died and was buried in a borrowed tomb. The Son of God was born from a virgin womb and buried in a virgin tomb. Christ Jesus voluntarily gave up His riches in glory in exchange for the poverty of mankind on earth. Grace comes at the great expense of Jesus giving up all for all people.

God's grace and forgiveness are the true riches. Any other riches that compete with Christ's riches are idols of insecurity. Indeed, it is better for us to be poor in the eyes of the world and remain rich in the eyes of our heavenly Father. It is futile and frustrating to chase the undependable wealth of the world, when we can rest and revel in the riches of seeking first the kingdom of God. Grace exhibits generosity.

⸺◦∞◦⸺

"Listen, my dear brothers and sisters: Has not God
chosen those who are poor in the eyes of the world
to be rich in faith and to inherit the kingdom he
promised those who love him?" (James 2:5).

Has pride in your socioeconomic status caused you to feel superior to those with less of this world's stuff? If so, your possessions have become a stumbling block to seeking God's kingdom first. Are you more fearful of losing your things than you are of losing the Lord's favor in your life? These false beliefs and behaviors cause cultural Christians to lose their luster for Christ. True riches come from Jesus alone.

It is better to be poor but rich in grace, than to be rich and poor in grace. However, a man or woman in poverty who is motivated by greed is much worse off than the rich who are generous in their charitable deeds and gifts. So, our priority is to follow the example of Jesus, not allowing material goods to master our coming and going. When we are free from financial trappings, we are free to trust the one worthy of our trust, Jesus Christ, whose simple life compels us to live uncomplicated lives for His kingdom's sake.

"A man said to [Jesus], 'I will follow you wherever you go.' Jesus replied, 'Foxes have dens and birds have nests, but the Son of Man has no place to lay his head'" (Luke 9:57-58).

Heavenly Father, teach me to seek You first, above any financial allurements.

Related Readings

Proverbs 28:6,11; 22:2; Luke 18:22; Revelation 3:17

43

Lord, Help Me

———— ⌘ ————

The woman came and knelt before him. "Lord, help me!" she said.

MATTHEW 15:25

A life lived well requires help from the Lord. Life is like a ship on open seas: we navigate through calm waters, rough waters, uncertain waters, and beautiful waters—but all the time trusting its Creator. The source of our strength must be Christ, or we are chronically tired. Faith in the Lord triumphs over fear and frustration. This is especially true when someone we love suffers severely and all we can do is lift them up to Jesus.

Indeed, His help happens to those who kneel in humble dependency and cry out to Jesus, "Lord, help me!" When the body writhes in pain, we cry for help. When a critical word crushes our spirit, we cry for help. When unanswered questions stalk our mind, we cry for help. When relational conflict emaciates our emotions, we cry for help. Help from heaven gives hope, healing, and the energy to push through tough times and trust Him.

———— ⌘ ————

"The LORD is my strength and my shield;
my heart trusts in him, and he helps me.
My heart leaps for joy,
and with my song I praise him" (Psalm 28:7).

His help gives joy where laughter has left. His help gives confidence in the middle of crisis. His help offers forgiveness when hurt has severed another's trust. His help harnesses grace and bridles a toxic tongue. His help reaches to the poorest of the poor, the richest of the rich, and everyone in between—with His saving grace in Jesus Christ.

How can Jesus help you? Do you need wisdom? Ask Him with a humble heart, and He will hear and answer your request. His response may come in the form of godly friends who give you wise advice—so look around and listen intently—for the Lord speaks through those who truly love you. Jesus helps those who humbly seek out and trust wise counsel.

———◦∞◦———

"When a mocker is punished, the simple gain wisdom;
by paying attention to the wise they get
knowledge" (Proverbs 21:11).

Who do you know that needs the Lord's help? Have you, on bended knee, petitioned Jesus on their behalf? Be bold for their sake and for the glory of God. Go to Jesus so someone can find Jesus's healing and forgiveness. Be an advocate for others.

———◦∞◦———

"May the Lord grant that he will find mercy from
the Lord on that day" (2 Timothy 1:18).

What help do I need from the Lord? On whose behalf can I seek help from the Lord?

Related Readings

Psalms 30:2,10; 33:20; Isaiah 41:13-14; Acts 20:35; Hebrews 13:6

44

Fruit of Repentance

⸻❧⸻

*Produce fruit in keeping with repentance…every tree that does not
produce good fruit will be cut down and thrown into the fire.*

A life surrendered to the Lord produces fruit of repentance. As a
well-kept vineyard is seasonally tilled and meticulously weeded,
so a Spirit-filled life is watered with grace, love, and mercy. Character
cultivation happens to a heart turned toward heaven, captivated by
trust in Jesus. Hailstorms damage or destroy the best-kept crops, but
the sun's life-giving rays and the nurturing farmer bring them back. In
this way God nurtures a disciple into His hearty harvest.

Spiritual fruit from the past is no substitute for fruit produced in
the present. Praise God for our faithful ancestors of the faith, but their
fruit was for their time. The Spirit of God looks to harvest fruit of
repentance for this generation. The good old days of spiritual renewal
are inspiring to reminisce on, but today the Lord calls those of us with
a little gray hair to grow up in His grace. We who identify with Jesus
have a significant role and responsibility to produce fruit of repentance.

⸻❧⸻

"I preached that they should repent and turn
to God and demonstrate their repentance
by their deeds" (Acts 26:20).

How do we know if we produce fruit of repentance? Private belief
for salvation and public confession in baptism are the first fruits of
repentance, but they are only the beginning. The ongoing fruit-bearing
process is a lifetime of leaning into the Lord. The Spirit reminds us
when we drift into bad habits or wrong thinking. We confess spiritual

pride and remember that only by the grace of God can we do good. We turn from self-righteousness and turn to God's righteousness.

What is the proof of fruit produced by repentance? Good deeds from a heart of humility and grace are fruits that glorify God. Your Spirit-filled actions of abstinence, generosity, tutoring, public service, faith sharing, foster care, and orphan adoption please your heavenly Father. Jesus smiles when you are hospitable and when you visit the sick and those in prison. Your authentic repentance keeps you broken so you may better care for the broken. What breaks God's heart breaks your heart!

——— ✺ ———

"Godly sorrow brings repentance that leads to salvation and leaves no regret, but worldly sorrow brings death" (2 Corinthians 7:10).

Heavenly Father, I repent of known and unknown sin in my heart. I turn to Your heart for forgiveness and the faith to produce good deeds.

Related Readings

Deuteronomy 4:30; Jeremiah 18:11; Ezekiel 47:12; Acts 11:18; Galatians 3:7

45

Share Extra Stuff

⸺◦⸺

*Anyone who has two shirts should share with the one who
has none, and anyone who has food should do the same.*

LUKE 3:11

Those with nothing need those with more, and those with more need to be generous with those with nothing. Our love for the Lord does not let us sit still when another needy soul is without. We pray for a need to be met, but we also offer our stuff in answer to our prayers. Like a holy offering to God, we place our stuff on His altar of compassion. Christ can entrust more to those who hold an open hand. Our life is a canal for cargo ships of care to carry our stuff to others.

Instead of complaining of a neighbor's unkempt yard, consider anonymous care. Invest in a monthly bus or train ticket for a friend who needs transportation to look for a job. Take the children of an out-of-work family to buy school clothes and supplies. Create work around your house or at your work that gives others opportunity to work. Look up your local food bank and become a volunteer or contributor. Share your extra possessions in Jesus's name.

⸺◦⸺

"Is it not to share your food with the hungry
and to provide the poor wanderer with shelter—
when you see the naked, to clothe them,
and not to turn away from your own
flesh and blood?" (Isaiah 58:7).

Helping hands are heaven's call for those who have extra. How can we enjoy self-indulgence and ignore one who has none? Thus, we give gas gift certificates to someone so they can travel to visit a friend.

Maybe for every bottle of water we consume, we provide a bottle of water for a child where water is not easily accessible. For every pair of shoes we buy, we provide a pair of shoes for another barefoot believer. Those with none need our extra some.

You could match every dollar a person invests to pay down their debt. Use your small investment in another to leverage a large feeling of being loved. A little bit of encouragement may be all someone needs to not give up and to keep going for God. Jesus gave His all, so we could be forgiven of all. Those with none need those with some!

—⌇⌇⌇—

"I needed clothes and you clothed me, I was
sick and you looked after me, I was in prison
and you came to visit me" (Matthew 25:36).

Heavenly Father, lead me by Your Spirit to give my some to those with none.

Related Readings

Job 31:19-20; Isaiah 16:4; Ezekiel 18:16; Luke 10:33-37;
    Hebrews 13:2

46

Extravagant Love Pursues

———— ∞ ————

Suppose one of you has a hundred sheep and loses one of
them. Doesn't he leave the ninety-nine in the open country
and go after the lost sheep until he finds it? And when he
finds it, he joyfully puts it on his shoulders and goes home.

LUKE 15:4-6

God never gives up on His lost sheep. He pursues them with an extravagant and passionate love that exceeds human understanding. The secluded and insecure sheep trembles in fear and worry, but the Great Shepherd gently picks them up. He places them on the broad shoulders of His salvation. His eyes of compassion create comfort, and His heart of forgiveness brings joy. Jesus the Shepherd of our soul never stops loving us or pursuing us in our sin.

Do you feel lost and alone? Have you wandered from the care of Christ into the discomfort of some bad decisions? If so, you are not the first one to find yourself unsure of what to do next and embarrassed about your precarious predicament. You may have drifted from God's best for now, but you do not have to remain in this scary state of mind. Your heavenly Father is hot on your heels with His loving-kindness and long-suffering. Ask Him to hoist you onto His back.

———— ∞ ————

"We all, like sheep, have gone astray,
each of us has turned to our own way;
and the LORD has laid on him
the iniquity of us all" (Isaiah 53:6).

Who do you know who needs the pursuit of your extravagant love? Perhaps a child who is lost in the weeds of the world but longs for your unconditional acceptance. Or a colleague who has failed, but with the assurance of your trust and encouragement will try again. Maybe your spouse is experiencing a life change or a midlife crisis. They desperately desire your grace and patience. Pursue those who are on the edge of despair. Love them back to the support of saints.

Most of all enjoy the grace of God's goodness. His extravagant love goes with you in your ups and downs. He leads you with the staff of His Holy Spirit. He teaches you with the wisdom of His Word. He uplifts you with the joy of Jesus. He corrects you with His loving discipline. He carries you when you are exhausted and unsure what to do next. Yes, celebrate with Christ the joy of your salvation and the event of one sinner who repents. His extravagant love seeks you!

"For 'you were like sheep going astray,' but
now you have returned to the Shepherd and
Overseer of your souls" (1 Peter 2:25).

Heavenly Father, thank You for pursuing me with Your
extravagant love and grace.

Related Readings
Numbers 27:17; Ezekiel 34:5; Matthew 9:36; Mark 6:34; John 10:11

47

Jesus, the Intercessor

He is also able to save to the uttermost those who come to God through Him, since He always lives to make intercession for them.

HEBREWS 7:25 NKJV

Jesus sits at the right hand of His Father, ever interceding on behalf of His followers. Because of His sinless sacrifice for the human race, followed by His glorious resurrection, He is qualified to mediate between God and man. Christ is positioned in heaven to help all who call on His name. Indeed, just as He selflessly served as the Son of man, so He still serves in heaven on behalf of His servants on earth. Jesus is an advocate to Almighty God for those who need mercy and grace.

Praise God, our heavenly Father looks over to His Son Jesus instead of looking down on unholy human beings. In Christ, the Lord sees forgiveness, not guilt. He sees sinlessness, not sin. He sees acceptance, not rejection. He sees life, not death. He sees wisdom, not foolishness. He sees healing, not hurt. He sees grace, not law. He sees mercy, not judgment. He sees love, not hate. Yes, we have entered into a covenant relationship with Christ, and He represents us to God in purity.

"Who then is the one who condemns? No one.
Christ Jesus who died—more than that, who
was raised to life—is at the right hand of God
and is also interceding for us" (Romans 8:34).

Where do you struggle? Who has hurt you? Lay your sorrows, fears, and pain at the feet of Jesus, and He will represent your needs to your loving heavenly Father. Don't concern yourself with what might be appropriate or inappropriate to ask of the Lord, because Jesus filters your prayer requests in His righteous wisdom. He will only give over to God what is worthy of the grace of God. Yes, Christ weighs the motive of your heart before He presents your request to God.

Therefore, petition Jesus with bold belief from a pure heart. When you are unsure what to request in prayer, trust Christ to communicate to your heavenly Father on your behalf. Most of all listen to the Lord and what the Spirit is saying to your spirit. The closer you walk with Christ, the closer your will aligns with His will. Prayer becomes a quiet affirmation from the Holy Spirit as you become one with Jesus. Hallelujah, He lives in heaven and appears for you in God's presence!

❧

> "Christ did not enter a sanctuary made with human hands that was only a copy of the true one; he entered heaven itself, now to appear for us in God's presence" (Hebrews 9:24).

Heavenly Father, thank You for giving me Jesus as my personal intercessor at Your throne of grace and mercy.

Related Readings

Job 16:20; Isaiah 53:12; 1 Timothy 2:5; 1 John 2:1

48

Be with Jesus

—⊗⊗⊗—

He appointed twelve that they might be with him
and that he might send them out to preach.

MARK 3:14

First and foremost, Jesus calls His children to be with Him. A disciple's devotion to God precedes his or her duty for God. His first task is ministering to the heart of the mission-minded disciple. Otherwise, the primary goal becomes executing the mission of the Lord. Obedience is critical, but not before receiving the love of Jesus. Intimacy defines compliance to His commands with grace. Solitude with the Savior prepares a disciple to serve.

Yes, our primary call is to be with God on earth before we go to be with Him in heaven. Sweet communion with Christ sustains our public zeal for His great commission of disciple-making. We go into the world to make disciples after the Holy Spirit molds us into spirit-filled followers through intimate prayer. As we experience the Lord's greatest command to love and be loved by Him, we are ready for His great commission to make disciples. Be with Jesus to share Jesus!

—⊗⊗⊗—

"'You do not want to leave too, do you?' Jesus asked
the Twelve. Simon Peter answered him, 'Lord, to
whom shall we go? You have the words of eternal
life. We have come to believe and to know that
you are the Holy One of God'" (John 6:67-69).

We are tempted to turn our backs on Jesus when it is too hard or too easy. It may feel too hard because nothing seems to work—our prayers remain unanswered, our relationships teeter on the rocks, and our finances are a wreck. We want to give up on God because He does not give us what we need. Or, life may be really good for now, so we feel the freedom to be free from real faithfulness to God. Our prayers can become perfunctory and our obedience an obligation.

However, whether times are hard or easy, we still need our time with Jesus. We need to be with Jesus because our souls remain needy regardless of our external failures or successes. The Lord loves to walk with us through our valleys and to our mountaintops, and most times the good and the bad things in life happen simultaneously. We go to be with Jesus because no one else has words of eternal life. We want to be with Him in love so we can go out and love others for Him!

"Dear friends, let us love one another, for love
comes from God. Everyone who loves has been
born of God and knows God" (1 John 4:7).

Heavenly Father, my heart longs to be with You so I can best love for You.

Related Readings
Hosea 3:1; Matthew 11:28; Mark 6:31; Romans 1:7; Galatians 2:20

49

Children Praise God

*"Do you hear what these children are saying?" they asked him.
"Yes," replied Jesus, "have you never read,
'From the lips of children and infants
you, Lord, have called forth your praise'?"*

MATTHEW 21:16

The Lord calls forth praise from the lips of precious children to Him. They praise Him for they know He loves them. They praise Him because He cares for them. They praise Him for His goodness. They praise Him for His forgiveness. They praise Him for the beauty of His holiness. Their praise is pure, unsoiled by skeptics. A child has yet to be defiled by the cynical sorts Satan sends to confuse adults. Their authentic air of worship drifts a pleasing aroma into the nostrils of God.

A child is positioned by their honest intentions and trusting hearts to embrace Jesus Christ as their Savior and Lord. Thus, as parents we are responsible to encourage their growth in grace and truth. We teach them songs of praise at an early age so words of worship make their way into the depths of their moldable hearts. "Bless the Lord, O my soul, and all that is within me" will not be soon forgotten by a son or daughter who sings this to Jesus. Yes, praise revels in Christ's salvation.

"The living, the living—they praise you,
as I am doing today;
parents tell their children
about your faithfulness" (Isaiah 38:19).

Furthermore, make it fun for your child to praise Jesus. Play uplifting and joyful music in the car and at home. A simple chorus, such as

"Obedience is the very best way to show that you believe," is an easy phrase to recall, and it reflects the heart of Christ. He says, "If you love me, keep my commands" (John 14:15). A simple and appropriate way for a child to honor their parents is to obey them. Instant obedience is an indicator of a person whose praise to God is life-changing.

A family who worships together grows in grace together. Yes, there are times you wonder if all the Sunday morning ruckus is worth the physical energy and emotional stress to get your little ones to church. Absolutely! Keep your family in a healthy, faith-filled environment. As a greenhouse grows luscious fruit and vegetables, so your child's heart warms to God in worship. Encourage your child to praise God by your passionate praise to God. He inhabits His praises!

"But thou art holy, O thou that inhabitest
the praises of Israel" (Psalm 22:3 KJV).

Heavenly Father, I praise You for Your goodness, humility, and mercy. May I praise You with the purity of a child.

Related Readings

Exodus 15:2; Psalms 8:2; 71:22; Luke 10:21; 1 Corinthians 1:26-29

50

Evil Intent Exposed

―――――∽∞∽―――――

"Tell us then, what is your opinion?
Is it right to pay the imperial tax to Caesar or not?"
But Jesus, knowing their evil intent, said, "You
hypocrites, why are you trying to trap me?"

MATTHEW 22:17-18

Beware of those with evil intent. Their motivation is to make others look bad so they can look good. Unscrupulous individuals seek to weaken another's authority so they can step into the power vacuum and take control. They use flattery to gain favor from their victim. They acquire trust so they can discredit their opponent's character. A heart with evil intent uses truth to set a trap of confusion. Thus, wisdom and discernment are required to confront confusion with clarity.

Has another attempted to question your character? Have you answered their clever questions directly with insight from Scripture? Pray the Holy Spirit reveals the heart of God to your heart, so you righteously respond to unrighteous inquiries. Questions with evil intent are fishing for an evil reaction, but in the power of the Holy Spirit, you don't have to lower yourself to acting like your agitators. Be bold but respectful. Be direct but with grace and truth.

―――――∽∞∽―――――

"But I tell you, love your enemies and pray for
those who persecute you" (Matthew 5:44).

Furthermore, pray for those in authority who use others to do their dirty work. They take advantage of subordinates who wish to avoid trouble. Thus, we don't shoot the messenger, but by God's grace we grow in our compassion and empathy for their no-win situation.

Perhaps they fear losing their boss's approval, or they don't want to jeopardize their promotion—so they give in to being used. So, be like Joseph and his jailer: Seek God's favor and serve. You may gain more influence for Christ.

Finally, guard your heart if you feel betrayed, attacked, dismissed, or marginalized. Let go of hurt and be healed. Release anger and forgive. Lovingly confront critics with grace and truth. When you feel wronged, pray for the Holy Spirit to give you the right words with the right spirit. The battle is the Lord's, so you can trust Him to deal with evil intent in His timing. Trust in the Lord with all your heart, so your heart is free from fear and retaliation. He exposes evil intent.

—∞—

> "For the eyes of the Lord are on the righteous and
> his ears are attentive to their prayer, but the face of
> the Lord is against those who do evil" (1 Peter 3:12).

Heavenly Father, give me Your heart to lovingly confront another's evil intent with grace and truth.

Related Readings
1 Samuel 12:19; Psalm 141:5; John 17:15; 2 Thessalonians 3:2

51

Protect Your Family

⸻

An angel of the Lord appeared to Joseph in a dream. "Get up," he said, "take the child and his mother and escape to Egypt. Stay there until I tell you, for Herod is going to search for the child to kill him."

MATTHEW 2:13

The Lord protects His children. He protects them from those with evil intent. He reveals the unrighteous motives of unscrupulous men and women. He protects His loved ones from temptation. But when they are tempted, He provides a way of escape. He protects His followers from themselves. He surrounds them with objective counsel. Wise ones tell them what they need to hear in love, not what they want to hear. God protects what is precious to His heart.

There are defining moments that require the prayerful protection of our family. It may be a financial temptation to borrow too much money. This materialistic burden forces us to work too much to the neglect of our spouse and children. Instead, a contented heart rejects detrimental desires to live beyond our means. Perhaps our family needs us to radically curtail the calendar so we are free to be a family. We can live under God's protection in order to rest in Him.

⸻

"May integrity and uprightness protect me,
because my hope, LORD, is in you" (Psalm 25:21).

Moreover, your integrity is an instrument of the Lord's protection. Your good name is like an imposing cast-iron security gate that the enemy cannot scale. Your character is a thick-walled citadel of Christ's protection that rests on the hill of His help. Like money, the worth of your integrity compounds over time. It protects you from people assuming the worst. Instead they assume the best. Your integrity protects your family.

Furthermore, your heavenly Father protects you with His love and faithfulness. The goodness of God, like a fortified castle, provides safety from unseemly souls. His love leads you only to places where He is with you. His faithfulness does not falter. Nations may fail to pay their debts, but the Lord God Almighty is 100 percent dependable. Thus, keep your family trusting in Jesus. When your family is under God's authority, they are under His protection. His grace guards your home!

"May he be enthroned in God's presence forever;
appoint your love and faithfulness
to protect him" (Psalm 61:7).

Heavenly Father, lead me into Your protection and away from my impulsive actions.

Related Readings

Joshua 24:17; Psalms 12:5,7; 20:1; 91:14; Malachi 2:16;
    2 Thessalonians 3:3

52

Approachable Jesus

———— ∞ ————

Another time Jesus was praying,
and when He finished, one of His disciples approached Him.
Disciple: "Teacher, would You teach us Your way of prayer?"

LUKE 11:1 VOICE

Jesus is approachable to all who desire His company. God did not create the earth like a watch, winding it up and then stepping back to let it run without His intervention. No, the Lord is personal and approachable. He invites His children to ask honest questions about how to pray, how to love, how to forgive, and how to give. Yes, He loves to engage and instruct in His ways. Jesus moves the mind with clear teaching and captures the heart with riveting and relevant stories.

A disciple who walked with Jesus on earth struggled with his prayers to heaven. He watched Jesus pray, but the student still needed some direction. So, even today as we grow in our faith, we need the Holy Spirit to reveal to us the ways of God. We are disciples who sincerely want to know how to live for the Lord. He is not shy in showing us what to say and how to serve. Just as we love giving to our children, God loves to give His Spirit to all who ask.

———— ∞ ————

"At Gibeon the LORD appeared to Solomon during
the night in a dream, and God said, 'Ask for
whatever you want me to give you'" (1 Kings 3:5).

Are you approachable? Do others feel the freedom to seek your counsel and ideas? When people see the fruit of your character they want to ask you about how you live life. As you lovingly lead others, learners will want to know why you lead so unselfishly. Questions are your opportunity to point people back to the Lord's love for you and your reciprocal approach to leading others. Tell stories of your struggles to lead in love and how you grew in grace over time. Invite questions.

Approachability is the outcome of acceptance. When your children, grandchildren, friends, and coworkers know you accept them for who they are, they will want to know who you are. Your unconditional acceptance of someone is an invitation to love them for Jesus's sake. Lastly, approach the Lord often with your fears, dreams, and desires. He delights in your prayers and unleashes His Spirit to all who call on His name. Humbly approach Him and expect to be loved!

"Let us then approach God's throne of grace with confidence, so that we may receive mercy and find grace to help us in our time of need" (Hebrews 4:16).

Heavenly Father, thank You for receiving me just as I am and answering my questions concerning my struggles.

Related Readings
Exodus 20:21; Ephesians 2:18; 3:12; Hebrews 7:19; 1 John 4:17; 5:14

53

Humble and Gentle

"After me comes the one more powerful than I, the straps of whose sandals I am not worthy to stoop down and untie"...Just as Jesus was coming up out of the water, he saw heaven being torn open and the Spirit descending on him like a dove.

MARK 1:7,10

Jesus was introduced by a humble man and a gentle dove. One came from earth as reminder of the need for our confession of sins, and the other came from heaven as a reminder of God's forgiveness of sins. City and country people came to be cleansed of their sin. Spiritual revival spread like fire across the villages and into the towns, as John and Jesus were lightning rods for the Holy Spirit's energy. Indeed, their humble and gentle attitudes invited the Trinity's trust and favor.

We are drawn to preachers and teachers who proclaim and teach truth from a humble heart and a gentle spirit. Truth is convicting enough without the pride of man adding insult to injury. With humility we can say something hard with a smile and still solicit the trust of our friend. Our gentle words carry with them the blessing of God's Spirit. Humble men and women point people to Jesus, not to themselves. Gentleness turns people to God. It's here they feel His love and approval.

"Take my yoke upon you and learn from me, for I am gentle and humble in heart, and you will find rest for your souls" (Matthew 11:29).

Do you submit to God moment by moment so the fullness of His Spirit bears the fruit of humility and gentleness in your life? Union with your Lord brings out His best in You. Because He is gentle, you become gentle. Since He is humble, you become humble. You grow in support of your relationships by being available to satisfy their needs. Patience is your fuel for gentleness, and prayer powers your humility. Your heavenly Father is well pleased when you grow in His attributes.

God graced the globe with a gentle and peaceful dove. We feel His love, just as He pronounced His pleasure for His Son Jesus. Like Noah, who knew the storms were over when the dove's beak clenched an olive branch, Jesus was God's olive branch to mankind's mishaps. Grace is God's rainbow of redemption to our fear-flooded world. Glory in the salvation of a forgiving Trinity. Rejoice, for we are invited into the humble and gentle community of the Father, Son, and Spirit!

"Rejoice greatly, Daughter Zion!
Shout, Daughter Jerusalem!
See, your king comes to you,
righteous and victorious,
lowly and riding on a donkey"
(Zechariah 9:9).

Lord Jesus, grow my spirit by the power of Your humble and gentle Spirit.

Related Readings

Genesis 8:11; Joel 2:28; Acts 11:16; Ephesians 4:2; Colossians 3:2

54

Transformational Teaching

*When the Sabbath came, Jesus went into the synagogue and
began to teach. The people were amazed at his teaching,
because he taught them as one who had authority.*

MARK 1:21-22

Jesus's teaching was like no one else's—clear, compelling, authoritative, and based on Himself, the living Word. He also explained the Scriptures with clarity and conviction in a way that caused demons to tremble and shriek, exiting the body of the one they possessed. The religious leaders were jealous of this new, younger teacher, whom they feared as competition. Jesus ministered the Word to crowds with His Holy Spirit–inspired teaching, and then loved them individually.

Transformational teaching handles the Word of God with humility. There is a reverence of God that points to Christ as the author and finisher of our faith. It's out of a loving relationship with the Living Word, Jesus, that we are able to compassionately communicate the written Word of God. As we love the Lord with our hearts and minds, our teaching engages the hearts and minds of our hearers. We should bow before God in prayerful preparation before we stand for God to teach.

"The Teacher sought to find just the right words to
express truths clearly" (Ecclesiastes 12:10 NLT).

We are challenged to walk afresh in faith and to invite His words to transform our lives by the power of the Holy Spirit. If you teach, teach what God has taught you—one broken person to another. Speak openly where the Lord has brought you. Exhort and teach transparently out of your weakness, and Christ will show Himself strong. What you teach instructs and inspires, but how you live is a transformational model for others to follow.

As students, we are wise to sit under the teaching of teachers who instruct from the authority of God's Word. However, make sure to learn from those whose hearts and minds are engaged with Christ's heart and mind. Learn from men and women who have been transformed on their knees in humble prayer by God, before they sit behind their desks to prepare themselves to teach. Transformational teaching comes from the Spirit's conviction and instruction. Learn from Him!

"Let my teaching fall like rain
and my words descend like dew,
like showers on new grass,
like abundant rain on tender
plants" (Deuteronomy 32:2).

Heavenly Father, transform my heart by Your transformational teaching inspired by Your Spirit and modeled by Your servants.

Related Readings

Psalm 78:1; Isaiah 2:3; John 14:24; Acts 18:11; Hebrews 5:12

55

Life's Interruptions

*Simon and his companions went to look for him, and when they
found him, they exclaimed: "Everyone is looking for you!"*

MARK 1:36-37

Life is full of interruptions. Car maintenance, a sick child, divorce, death, financial surprises, a friend's crisis, government shutdowns, home repair, health questions, and job issues all can interrupt our regular routine. If we have perfectionistic tendencies, we can stress out when we lose control, or we can learn to embrace that Christ is in control. Ironically, expectations of a stress-free life only create stress. As long as we live, life will interrupt…so how shall we respond?

Jesus was interrupted in His prayers, and He was interrupted by the leper, but He used both for God's glory. Is the Lord in on our life's interruptions? Many times, yes! He takes distractions in our prayer time and uses them to lead us into His will. On occasion during prayer, my mind will race with a mental list that longs for immediate attention. So I stop praying, write down the items, and then offer the list in prayer as a sacrifice to Jesus. The Holy Spirit leads me in how to meet the needs I've written down. So I seek to lean into the Lord when interrupted by life.

"Instead, you ought to say, 'If it is the Lord's will,
we will live and do this or that'" (James 4:15).

We are all needy to one degree or another. Needy people need their needs to be met, so when someone interrupts your life with a need, look for the Lord in the interruption. Pray for a way to meet their need in Jesus's name, so they are attracted to His love. Furthermore, you are not called to meet everyone's needs all the time. There are others God wants to engage, as His benevolent blessing. Be available, do what you can, and trust the Lord to provide the resources.

First we must seek Christ Jesus to meet all our needs in Him. His love, His patience, His mercy, His rest, and His care are a treasure trove of spiritual invigoration, emotional healing, and mental stamina. The Lord is with us in the middle of life's interruptions. Don't forget to seek those who love us when we need love. Ask for prayer in your pain. We need each other, and we need our Savior Jesus when life interrupts our plans. Yes, life's interruptions direct us to God's better plan!

—⊗⊗⊘—

"My God will meet all your needs according to the riches of his glory in Christ Jesus" (Philippians 4:19).

Heavenly Father, when life interrupts my goals and aspirations, thank You for meeting my needs in Christ Jesus.

Related Readings
Psalms 23:1; 39:5; Matthew 8:24; Luke 12:18-20; 2 Corinthians 9:8

56

Influence of Impure Spirits

―――――∞∞∞―――――

*Just then a man in their synagogue who was possessed by an impure
spirit cried out, "What do you want with us, Jesus of Nazareth?"*

MARK 1:23-24

There are impure spirits inside some people. Some even possess individuals in our places of worship. It is scary to see those who have Satan as their master and who are set on disrupting the work of God. They may say they believe in God, because "even the demons believe and tremble," but their heart is far from Him. Impure spirits try to blend in with true believers, but they are exposed as fakes to those with spiritual discernment. Christ's presence drives them out.

Jesus encountered evil in the synagogue and cast out an impure spirit from a man. Demons are not comfortable where Christ is taught and where the Spirit of God has a powerful presence. Unfortunately, some impotent churches have people who go through the motions with zombie-like spiritual energy. The enemy's influence has embedded their minds. Evil induces individuals to smile and be satisfied to live for themselves. Impure spirits lead people to live impure lives.

―――――∞∞∞―――――

"You believe that there is one God. Good! Even the
demons believe that—and shudder" (James 2:19).

Therefore, make sure to not make light of the influence of impure spirits. If you embrace activities and entertainment that espouse evil, you expose yourself and your family to the influence of impure spirits. Even events done in fun and jest can open the door to the unintentional consequences of accepting the abnormal as normal. Your children can dress up and have fun without imitating witches, warlocks, spiritists, and the occult. Why dance with the enemy and risk defilement by his influence?

Furthermore, pray against impure spirits in the pure name of Jesus Christ. They cannot stand it when we stand up to them in the mighty name of Jesus. Everyone will bow to our Lord Jesus.

> God exalted him to the highest place and gave him the name that is above every name, that at the name of Jesus every knee should bow, in heaven and on earth and under the earth, and every tongue acknowledge that Jesus Christ is Lord, to the glory of God the Father (Philippians 2:9-11).

Impure spirits cannot remain in the presence of ultimate purity, the Lord Jesus.

———— ⚬⚬⚬ ————

"Do not turn to mediums or seek out spiritists,
for you will be defiled by them. I am the
LORD your God" (Leviticus 19:31).

Heavenly Father, lead me by Your Spirit to discern impure spirits and confront them in the pure name of Jesus Christ.

Related Readings
1 Samuel 28:3-9; Job 1:6-12; Mark 3:15; 1 Timothy 4:1;
    Revelation 9:20

57

Emotional Jesus

When Jesus saw her weeping, and the Jews who had come along with
her also weeping, he was deeply moved in spirit and troubled.
"Where have you laid him?" he asked.
"Come and see, Lord," they replied.
Jesus wept.
Then the Jews said, "See how he loved him!"

JOHN **11:33-36**

Jesus felt deeply. He felt the intense sorrow of Mary and Martha losing their brother. He felt gratitude for friends and family who came
alongside to support them in their grief. His spirit was moved by the
trouble His loved ones experienced. Indeed, our Lord wept with those
who wept, and He rejoiced with those who rejoiced. He was much
more than the pale, emotionless, European portraits of the Renaissance.
Love feels deeply human needs.

Love takes the time to be with those who hurt and mourn over
loss. Love in action is emotion expressed. Friendship is a communica-
tion of affection. We are strong for the weak when we weep with them.
Unemotional responses to a hurting heart only prolong the healing.
Instead we can pray by the Holy Spirit to enter into emotional access
with our troubled friends and family. We love by being available. Love
emotionally connects.

"As he approached Jerusalem and saw the
city, he wept over it" (Luke 19:41).

What human condition deserves our empathy? Have we so insu-
lated ourselves from pain that we are numb to those who silently suffer?

Indeed, we are called by Christ to intentionally comfort the comfort-less. Others who grieve and wail from within need our supportive, tender compassion. Stealthily we can cook a meal, sit by a bedside and hold a hand, cradle a crying baby in our arms, hug a sobbing soul.

Are your emotions healthy enough for you to wholly love another soul? If not, invite the sweet salve of Jesus's comfort to free you to feel again. Under the Spirit's control, freely express what you feel: anger, fear, insecurity, disappointment, grief, or frustration. Feelings processed properly in prayer become helpful prescriptions for others stuck in sorrow. Learn the skills of emotional conversation, so you can help others locked up by unresolved pain. An expressive heart loves Jesus, so prayerfully speak what you feel. Jesus does.

"Jesus, full of joy through the Holy Spirit, said, 'I praise you, Father, Lord of heaven and earth'" (Luke 10:21).

Heavenly Father, thank You for the compassion and joy of Jesus. Help me to express my emotions in a healthy way.

Related Readings

Job 16:5; Psalm 100:2; Isaiah 63:9; Luke 6:23; Hebrews 12:2; Jude 1:24

58

Dare to Believe

⬢

*He said to her, "Daughter, your faith has healed you. Go
in peace and be freed from your suffering."*

MARK 5:33-34

At times our faith dares us to believe Jesus, to take Him at His word.
It may be unconventional, like the chronically ill woman who
suffered for 12 years. She was broke at the bank and broken in her heart.
Her last gasp of hope was to seek healing from the Great Healer. Like
her, on occasion, we feel our faith must press through life's circumstances to find the Lord. But once by faith we touch His merciful robe
of righteousness, His healing Spirit makes our spirit whole.

Jesus understands your concerns over rising healthcare costs and
the ability to take physical care of yourself and your family. Go to Him
for peace and a plan that works for you today, not stressing over the
what-ifs of tomorrow. By His grace through faith, let God bring wholeness to your soul and comfort to your body. The Lord's healing may
come through diet, doctors, and medication, or through an inexplica-
ble miracle of His intervention. Dare to believe in His power!

⬢

"Heal me, LORD, and I will be healed;
save me and I will be saved,
for you are the one I praise" (Jeremiah 17:14).

What life challenge are you facing that dares you to believe God?
Perhaps a prodigal child who continues to break your heart. Pray they
come to the end of themselves and become broken before God. Maybe
the fear of being alone ties your stomach up in knots. Let go of the lie
that the Lord will leave or forsake you; trust Him to lead you to those

who accept you. Dare to believe God. Press through your problems in faith, kneeling at Jesus's feet and telling Him your story.

Finally, ignore the noise of the crowd. Some may make fun of your faith or judge you for being bold, but those who love the Lord will love and encourage you in your walk with Christ. Those full of jealousy and insecurity will try to put you down, believing that doing so will lift them up. In spite of these misguided people, as you grow in your intimacy with Jesus, you will have the spiritual stamina to love naysayers to Christ. They'll experience your heart of mercy and sense you have been with Jesus! When you raise your bar of belief, others raise their bars. Dare to believe and others will believe.

⸎

"Be on your guard; stand firm in the faith;
be courageous; be strong. Do everything
in love" (1 Corinthians 16:13-14).

Heavenly Father, I pray for the courage to push through my circumstances and touch the mercy and power of Jesus.

Related Readings
1 Kings 3:6; Psalm 26:3; Mark 1:40; 11:22; Acts 27:25;
   Colossians 1:4-5

59

Misunderstood by Family

―∽∽∽―

*Jesus said to them, "A prophet is not without honor except in
his own town, among his relatives and in his own home."*

MARK 6:4

Jesus was at first misunderstood by His family and friends. "Once a
carpenter," they thought, "always a carpenter." Those He grew up
with had no category for Him becoming the Christ. Since He was one
of them, they wondered where His wisdom had come from. Therefore, be encouraged because Jesus encountered our same feelings of
misunderstanding and rejection from family. His response was prag-
matic: to move on from where He wasn't welcomed. Jesus went where
He was honored.

Our families do not always understand our faith in Jesus Christ.
They may be polite and offer a patronizing smile but then say disparag-
ing things behind our backs. Or they may say to our face that our faith
may be good for us, but not for them. Belief is a barrier for them. They
fear if they come to Christ, they will have to change. However, fear of
the Lord precludes other fears. His perfect love casts out the concerns
of those who need to receive His love. Our faith in Jesus remains pecu-
liar to people who remain in a state of unbelief in Jesus.

―∽∽∽―

"For whoever does the will of My Father in heaven is My
brother and sister and mother" (Matthew 12:50 NKJV).

Moreover, when those whose hearts are closed don't have ears to
hear, we move on to minister to those with open hearts. We still love
our unbelieving family members, but we do not allow their unbelief
to slow down our service for Jesus. We pray for them to experience the

light of the Lord's love as we proceed with Christ in the assurance of His will. Time is valuable, so we prayerfully look for opportunities to offer the gospel to receptive hearts and minds.

As you serve others in Jesus's name, consider going out in pairs. Serve with a friend so you have their prayer support. Seek to labor together, and ask Christ to protect you from unwise decisions. Minister with another friend for encouragement. Celebrate God's goodness together. Serve with another friend because Jesus said not to minister alone. Support your family in Jesus's name. Love them and share the gospel. One day, by faith, they may come to know Him. Pray misunderstandings move to understanding and to their acceptance of Christ as their Lord and Savior!

"'Now please forgive the sins of the servants
of the God of your father.'
When their message came to him,
Joseph wept" (Genesis 50:17).

Heavenly Father, use me to minister to my family even when they don't understand my faith walk or Your great love for them.

Related Readings

Nehemiah 1:6; Matthew 6:14; Acts 10:2; Ephesians 4:17-19

60

Timing Is Everything

Jesus warned them not to tell anyone about him.

MARK 8:30

Timing is everything. It is the difference between a strike and a home run in baseball. It determines if a cake is perfectly baked or dry and hard. Timing in conversation can solicit receptivity or invite defensiveness. It grows or hinders relationships. When and how we move forward with a decision to change determines the degree of its success. Timing definitely matters. Speaking the truth works best when anger has subsided and hearts are comforted. Prayer leads to the right time.

Jesus knew when His disciples and their audience could not yet handle the extent of who He was and what He was to do. They were ready to follow a reigning king but unprepared for a Savior who suffered and died. In the same way, we as modern-day disciples are fast to follow our risen Savior but slow to follow our suffering Savior. However, both are required for us to be authentic followers of Jesus. We truly follow our Lord once we are abandoned to Him.

"As they were coming down the mountain, Jesus instructed them, 'Don't tell anyone what you have seen, until the Son of Man has been raised from the dead'" (Matthew 17:9).

Seek God's perfect timing, whether at home or work. Have you prayerfully prepared your heart to comfort and confront your child in love? Is your decision-making process in the workplace collaborative and infused with wise counsel? Even when your motives are pure, a mistimed decision can make for an ugly outcome. Better to wait and work out the details before you offer an idea or plan. A mind that marinates in prayerful reflection gives the wisest response.

Always seek the Lord before a sensitive conversation with a friend or foe. Trust the Holy Spirit to lead you into His timing. Then when the time is right, be confident of what's right. Be like Peter at Pentecost—prepared, bold, and full of the Holy Spirit. Prayerfully proclaim the gospel of Christ to those the Lord brings into your life, those He has prepared beforehand. Now is the time—surrender to your risen Christ Jesus and embrace your suffering Savior!

"Don't waste your time on a scoffer;
all you'll get for your pains is abuse.
But if you correct those who care about life,
that's different—they'll love you
for it!" (Proverbs 9:8 MSG).

Heavenly Father, I trust in Your timing. You will lead me into Your will and way for my life.

Related Readings
Habakkuk 2:3; Matthew 26:18; Luke 1:20; 1 Corinthians 4:5

61

Inclusive, Not Exclusive

―――――∞∞∞―――――

*"Do not stop him," Jesus said. "For no one who does a
miracle in my name can in the next moment say anything
bad about me, for whoever is not against us is for us."*

Mark 9:39-40

The disciples debated who was the greatest based on their experiences with Jesus. Ambition and power drove them to want great positions in the coming kingdom. However, Jesus confronted their egos and put them in their place by calling them to serve. He defined greatness as being a servant to all. Christ is inclusive in His call to care for humanity's needs.

The disciples also struggled with religious pride. They told a stranger to cease ministry in Jesus's name because the perceived competitor was not part of their group. Jesus, on the other hand, urged His followers not to slow down works done in His name. He sanctioned them as good. A cease and desist to these good deeds for His sake was like tying a big rock around the neck of a child and causing them to drown. Other kingdom workers need to be empowered, not stopped. We are to support, not exclude, others outside our denomination who minister in Jesus's name.

―――――∞∞∞―――――

"Moses replied, 'Are you jealous for my sake? I wish
that all the Lord's people were prophets and that the
Lord would put his Spirit on them!'" (Numbers 11:29).

Our particular belief system is not a stick for beating others into submission. Nor can we expect them to conform to our way of doing ministry. If someone is not a part of our evangelical group, we are not to automatically suspect their unique ministry methods and beliefs. Jesus is inclusive, not exclusive, with groups who give Him the glory. As long as ministries and churches embrace Christ's deity and His death and resurrection for our sins, we have much in common.

Each legitimate Christian group has their own distinctive emphasis. Our motive is to encourage and empower other Jesus followers in their ministry. A unified body of Christ is inclusive in its makeup and its ministry to the world. Our risen Savior Jesus is our rallying cry for those lost in their sin and sorrow. Grace includes all who hunger for God's love!

"What I received I passed on to you...that Christ died for our sins according to the Scriptures, that he was buried, that he was raised on the third day according to the Scriptures" (1 Corinthians 15:3-4).

Heavenly Father, I accept and seek to emulate Your example of humble service. Help me to support all who call on Jesus's name.

Related Readings

Isaiah 42:6; Luke 2:32; Acts 8:9-25; 15:19,41; 26:23

62

Enemies of Jesus

⎯⎯⎯✿⎯⎯⎯

I tell you, love your enemies and pray for those who persecute you.

MATTHEW 5:44

Enemies of Jesus are ever looking for ways to dismiss, discredit, and destroy Him. Like the lost religious leaders of His day, they want to drive Christ out of their presence. The agnostic intellectuals of today dismiss Christ as a crutch for their cultured conscience. Contemporary theologically liberal leaders try to discredit Jesus's miracles as mere myth. Proud atheists seek to justify their godless behavior by destroying the absolutes that accompany God's existence.

The sad news is that those who seek to drive God out of culture are unable to simultaneously seek the good news of Jesus Christ. Enemies of the Lord do not know and understand Him. However, faithless attempts to flush faith from society tend to fuel that faith. Just as migratory birds move together toward a warmer climate before harsh weather arrives, so the faithful move closer to the warm heart of Christ when religious intolerance is tolerated. Enemies of Jesus may seem to be winning, but they'll soon be surprised they have lost their chance to seek Christ.

⎯⎯⎯✿⎯⎯⎯

"You are a child of the devil and an enemy of everything that is right! You are full of all kinds of deceit and trickery. Will you never stop perverting the right ways of the Lord?" (Acts 13:10).

A persecuted people of God is an opportunity to display the power of God. History proves that a church under fire is positioned to receive the Holy Spirit's fire. It's when the church blends in with the culture that it becomes irrelevant and impotent. So, praise God for the enemies of God. Their fight against faith demonstrates Christ's very power. It means freedom. Where freedom is, the Spirit takes up residence.

We who know Jesus must pray for the enemies of Jesus. We pray for them to seek to know Him, not ignore Him. We pray for them to seek to worship Him, not dismiss Him. We pray for them to seek to glorify Him, not discredit Him. We pray for them to seek to be saved by Him, not destroy Him. Lastly, fight the faithless with grace, love, and acceptance. The irresistible life of Jesus draws others to Jesus. Our surrendered life invites the enemy to commune with Christ.

"He has reconciled you by Christ's physical body through death to present you holy in his sight, without blemish and free from accusation" (Colossians 1:21-22).

Heavenly Father, teach me how to pray for Your enemies and model for them the life of Christ.

Related Readings

Psalm 74:10; Nahum 1:2; Matthew 5:44; Romans 5:10; James 4:4

63

Extraordinary Love Gives

∞∞∞

*She has done a beautiful thing to me…She did what she could. She
poured perfume on my body beforehand to prepare for my burial.*

MARK 14:6,8

Mary was overwhelmed by Christ's extraordinary love. He brought her brother Lazarus back to life, so she couldn't wait to express her love to Jesus. Her flesh and blood had been dead, but now he was alive again. Mary thought she had lost her brother until they would be reunited in eternity, but because of the compassion of Christ, he was back with her to enjoy more days together on earth. Yes, God's extraordinary love generously gives His children life and significance for living.

Thus, Mary did what she could to lavish love back on Jesus. She took her most valuable asset and gave it to her Lord. Unknowingly, she participated in God's will through the symbolic preparation of Christ's body for His death and burial. Simultaneously, she celebrated Lazarus's life and anointed Jesus for His forthcoming crucifixion for the sins of the world. Whose life can you celebrate who has passed from death to life in salvation? What remaining assets of yours can you dedicate to the proclamation of the gospel of Jesus Christ? Extraordinary love gives generously!

∞∞∞

"This is how much God loved the world: He gave
his Son, his one and only Son" (John 3:16 MSG).

Do we feel like Mary, overwhelmed with gratitude by the extraordinary love of Jesus? Perhaps a sibling who was dead in their sins has been forgiven and given new life in Christ. Maybe a parent in the twilight of life came to the end of themselves and said yes to Jesus as their Lord and Savior. Yes, we celebrate friends and family who were lost in their iniquities but have been made righteous by faith in Jesus Christ. He can forgive anyone and make them whole.

We can never pay back Jesus for His generous love, but we can express extraordinary love in His name for those who need life in Christ. By God's grace we dedicate our time, talent, and treasure for His kingdom. We anoint our assets with the precious oil of the Lord's lavish love in dedication to Him and His will. We prayerfully use our possessions to point people to Christ's sin-stained cross and empty tomb. Critics are silenced and made irrelevant by the extraordinary love that gives generously for God's glory. Love beautifully for Him!

———∞∞∞———

"How beautiful upon the mountains
Are the feet of him who brings good
news" (Isaiah 52:7 NKJV).

Heavenly Father, Your extraordinary love is beautiful to behold. Make my love extraordinary and beautiful to You.

Related Readings

Numbers 14:19; Nehemiah 1:5; Psalm 5:7; John 5:20; 19:40;
    1 John 3:1

64

God Provides

*He will show you a large room upstairs, furnished
and ready. Make preparations for us there.*

MARK 14:15

Often God's provision includes specific instructions of what we
need to do or not do. Jesus instructed His disciples to find a
man with a water pot and follow him to his master's house. The Lord
had already moved the heart of the generous master to have an upper
room prepared for Christ's work. Indeed, the Holy Spirit is at work all
around us in preparation for God's people. Often He uses people as a
channel for His provision. He blesses them to bless others.

First, listen intently to the Spirit's instruction before moving forward to discover where He is working. Patient prayer brings fulfillment. If we shortcut the Spirit's work, we strive in our own strength
and trade God's glory for our ego. Also, waiting gives other givers time
to share of their own wealth. Yes, God provides in His way, so we celebrate Christ's salvation!

∞∞

"Command those who are rich…to put their hope
in God, who richly provides us with everything
for our enjoyment" (1 Timothy 6:17).

Next, trust in God's provision to place the right people in your
path. We make one new relationship that leads to another resourceful
acquaintance, who has been praying about how they can support their
Savior's work. The Holy Spirit directs us as we move by faith from one
genuine God fearer to another. Like a multicolor, intricate tapestry, the

Lord's people are woven together on the loom of His love. The Spirit brings us together in a spirit of generosity for His purposes.

Most of all, place your hope in Christ, who richly provides you with everything for your enjoyment. Do not feel guilty because God gave you more than other good souls. Use your platform of belongings to brag on Jesus and be hilariously generous. You will find genuine joy in aggressive giving! Keep both hands open. Be a conduit for God's blessings. He provides for you so you may channel His gracious provision to others!

———∞∞∞———

"If anyone serves, they should do so with the
strength God provides" (1 Peter 4:11).

Heavenly Father, I trust You for Your provision in Your timing. Use my life to be a conduit of Your provision to other needy souls.

Related Readings

Exodus 15:22-27; Job 38:41; Luke 12:24; 1 Corinthians 10:31; Ephesians 6:10

65

Money's Betrayal

❦

*The betrayer had arranged a signal with them: "The one I kiss
is the man; arrest him and lead him away under guard."*

MARK 14:44

Money betrays with false promises and conflicting loyalties. Seductively, it lures in a once godly ambition and converts it into a scheme to secure cash at all costs. Even after we set firm boundaries between work and home, we can be tempted to ignore them when more money could be made. Someone can spend a lifetime consumed by accumulating wealth, only to lose their health and exhaust their net worth paying for their physical care. Judas betrayed a friend for financial gain. Beware of the love of money.

How do we know if we have been betrayed by money? How do we know if we are being betrayed for money? If our lifestyle has surpassed our modest means and handcuffed our home, we have been betrayed by money. If we worry more about owning stuff and status symbols, we have been betrayed by money. Moreover, we may be in the process of being exploited for money if our company or boss owns us. No margin for relationships, health, hobbies, emotions, family, and faith is a warning sign to slow down, stop, and objectively evaluate. Money betrays and steals.

❦

"One of his disciples, Judas Iscariot, who was
later to betray him, objected, 'Why wasn't this
perfume sold and the money given to the poor?
It was worth a year's wages'" (John 12:4-5).

Cash is the number one competitor for our devotion to Jesus Christ.

Some even spiritualize their intentions to get rich by declaring that one day they will have a benevolent heart—once they acquire excess cash. However, generosity is not governed by the amount given, but by the capacity to give. This is why a widow's mite means much more to God than a rich person who publicly tips the Lord only to be seen. The remedy to money's betrayal is generous living.

By God's grace we can release the unrighteous motivation to make money and embrace devotion to Jesus and generosity to our community. We've been directed to fear the Lord, not fear what people say, do, or think about us. The reality is, people think very little about us anyway. So if we die to self and stuff, we can live for Christ. We turn our backs on money's betrayal and turn to God and His loyalty.

—∽∾—

"Devise your strategy, but it will be thwarted;
propose your plan, but it will not stand,
for God is with us" (Isaiah 8:10).

Heavenly Father, I turn from money's betrayal and turn toward You, trusting in Your loyalty to me.

Related Readings

Psalm 118:6; Luke 12:18-21; 16:13; Acts 5:3-5; 1 Timothy 6:17-19; Hebrews 13:5

66

Emotional Manipulation

❦

"Do you want me to release to you the king of the Jews?"
asked Pilate, knowing it was out of self-interest that
the chief priests had handed Jesus over to him.

MARK 15:9-10

Emotional manipulation can be subtle or not so subtle. The Jewish leaders, in fear of losing their power, preyed on the fear of the crowd. In a mob like environment, jealous religious leaders manipulated the hearts of the masses to free the guilty and punish the innocent. Often fear is the favorite method of those who are afraid of losing control over people and circumstances. They use fear as an intimidation tool, wielding it like a billy club.

Beware of those who manipulate your emotional pain for their gain. People will use guilt to get your attention and coerce you to make a foolish decision in the moment. The pressure from peers needs to be filtered by your prayers. A friend's agenda is probably not the Lord's plan for your life. So allow the Spirit to calm your emotions and make His outlook clear. Holy Spirit persuasion trumps unholy spirit manipulation.

❦

"Shemaiah has prophesied to you, even
though I did not send him, and has persuaded
you to trust in lies" (Jeremiah 29:31).

On the other hand, it is good to be persuaded by the Holy Spirit and those filled with the Spirit. Listen to saints who love the Lord and learn from them. Be influenced by individuals of integrity, whose only goal is for you to enjoy God's game plan. That said, take time before trusting too quickly. If you crave a new friendship, you may want to share a confidence and hope for a reciprocal response. But maintain healthy expectations of others, and give people emotional space. Godly persuasion is patient.

In the power of the Holy Spirit, seek to persuade others of God's love for them and of the judgment to come. The fear of the Lord compels us to urge the unsaved to fear God. Jesus is King and Lord over all. His salvation is freedom from sin, self, and Satan. God's grace is good and life-giving. Our Lord has risen from the grave. He is alive, resurrected to save all who call on His name in repentance and faith. We persuade others because someone persuaded us. Emotional manipulation is temporary, but spiritual persuasion is eternal!

"Since, then, we know what it is to fear the Lord, we
try to persuade others" (2 Corinthians 5:11).

Heavenly Father, move my heart to persuade in the Spirit. Remind me not to push with my own strength.

Related Readings

Luke 20:45-47; Acts 28:23; Romans 4:21; Colossians 2:8;
2 Timothy 4:14-16

67

Shrewd for Jesus

⊶∞⊷

The master commended the dishonest manager because he had
acted shrewdly. For the people of this world are more shrewd in
dealing with their own kind than are the people of the light.

LUKE 16:8

Christians can be guilty of not being shrewd for Jesus. I can wrongly
presume that the Lord will take care of things without my best
efforts. On the contrary, Christ expects us to be as innocent as a dove
and as shrewd as a snake (Matthew 10:16). Gentleness and astuteness
go hand in hand. The gullible miss out on God's best, but the shrewd
know how to use God's wisdom. Engaged and mature thinkers consider creatively and calmly how to capitalize on a difficult situation.

Apathy breeds despair, and panic creates contempt. However, we
who know God have the mind of Christ. The Holy Spirit is our advocate, and His insights transcend conventional solutions during tough
times. The Spirit will lead us as we move forward by faith, but if we
remain immobile and anxious, we will fail. As children of the light we
have heavenly resources at our disposal. God's favor rests on us when
we attempt to influence people for His purposes.

⊶∞⊷

"Brothers and sisters, stop thinking like
children. In regard to evil be infants, but in your
thinking be adults" (1 Corinthians 14:20).

How do you use your resources to reach people for Jesus Christ?
One gauge of your effectiveness for the Lord is how well you make
friends who grow in their faith. People are attracted to your authen-
ticity and audacious faith. Bold risks breathed over in prayer become

trophies of God's grace and work. Use your business or work as a platform of creativity for Christ. Shun the status quo and lean into innovation. Last year's success needs this year's relevance.

Another suggestion: Do business with other believers who are excellent in their field. You support the economics of God's kingdom when you support other brothers and sisters in Christ. Christians will let you down, but learn how to work together and look for those whose values and maturity are similar to yours. Unite your community of faith around Christ. Use the talents of other Jesus followers to serve society, and in the process, you will build eternal dwellings!

───── ∞ ─────

"We know that if the earthly tent we live in is destroyed, we have a building from God, an eternal house in heaven, not built by human hands" (2 Corinthians 5:1).

Heavenly Father, give me Your wisdom to be shrewd for Jesus.

Related Readings

Exodus 1:10; Psalm 18:26; Ecclesiastes 11:1; Ephesians 5:8

68

Persistence Pays Off

Jesus told his disciples a parable to show them that
they should always pray and not give up.

LUKE 18:1

Has rejection caused you to give up on an opportunity or a person? Are you tired of trying to do the right thing, without experiencing positive results? It is precisely at this point of frustration and fear that God calls us to persevere in prayer and continue to graciously engage individuals and circumstances. Those who give up—give up on God.

Like an oscillating fan, your faith may waver back and forth between confidence and uncertainty, so hit the button of belief and stay focused on the Lord. Go forward by faith to encourage a relationship that didn't pan out. For example, call the company who went with a competitor and see how you might still serve them. Reach out until your requests are not ignored anymore.

A faithful man or woman in the hands of God has the attention of heaven and earth. When you are on His assignment, rejection has to first go through Almighty God's agenda. It's not the individual full of energy at the outset who outlasts others; it's the wise ones who conserve their vigor over the long haul—strengthened by their Savior's stamina.

∽◦∽

"To those who by persistence in doing
good seek glory, honor and immortality, he
will give eternal life" (Romans 2:7).

The fortitude of faith forges great relationships and gets long-term results. Anyone can start a race with excitement and anticipation, but few runners can climb the hills, overcome the adversity of the elements, and finish the course. You may not be the fastest—you may not finish first—but by God's grace you will finish well.

Most of all, stay persistent in prayer. Respond to God as the violin responds to the bow of the master. The Lord makes beautiful music on the strings of a life surrendered to Him. Persist through the pain of rejection by maintaining an attitude of prayer. Persistent prayer to Jesus produces His best outcome. Persistence pays off when you are prepared to move forward on behalf of your Master.

———— ⊶⊶ ————

"Rejoice always, pray continually, give thanks in
all circumstances; for this is God's will for you
in Christ Jesus" (1 Thessalonians 5:16-18).

What relationship or opportunity calls for my focused attention and persistence?

Related Readings

Numbers 14:38; Daniel 6:10; Acts 20:22-25; Romans 2:7

69

Compassion and Courage

---∞---

With a loud cry, Jesus breathed his last.

MARK 15:37

Christ's compassionate and courageous death on the cross gave immediate access to God for all who seek Him in faith. No more does a person need to go through a priest for God's forgiveness. Jesus is now the High Priest, and you have access to the Lord's forgiveness. Christ's death tore down the curtain to the most holy place, so all can be holy as He is holy. Jesus felt abandoned by God so sincere followers could abandon themselves to God. He became sin to forgive sin.

How do you express your gratitude to God for the compassion and courage of Christ for you? How do you access God through your High Priest Jesus in confession and repentance of sin? Sin is so serious that your heavenly Father sacrificed His only Son as payment for a debt you couldn't pay. A true confession is not conditional, nor does it make excuses. Instead, contrition courageously asks forgiveness, and by God's grace we can repent and find restitution.

---∞---

"God made him who had no sin to be sin
for us, so that in him we might become the
righteousness of God" (2 Corinthians 5:21).

A solitary soldier and many women who had supported Jesus's ministry remained with Him to the end. Little did they know it was just the beginning! The compassion and courage of the earliest Christ followers model for us how to follow Jesus. Society will ebb and flow in its interest in a Savior, but our passion intensifies as we receive His love. We stay engaged to support Christ's work, especially when others fall away.

Compassion and courage are staples for servants of Jesus. We seek out the spiritually lost, the emotionally bankrupt, and the physically displaced and invest our time and money in them for Christ's sake. Compassion is love in action, and courage carries it on the broad shoulders of bold belief. Obstacles are only stepping-stones for God, who proves Himself to be real and resourceful. Hence, continuous courage is fueled by faith in Christ. While others hide out in fear, we remain faithful.

———∞∞∞———

"This calls for patient endurance on the part of the people of God who keep his commands and remain faithful to Jesus" (Revelation 14:12).

Heavenly Father, fill me with the compassion and courage of Christ, so I may remain faithful to You.

Related Readings

Exodus 34:6; Joshua 1:7-9; 1 Corinthians 16:13-14; Colossians 3:12

70

God Keeps His Promises

❧

"Don't be alarmed," he said. "You are looking for Jesus the Nazarene, who was crucified. He has risen! He is not here."

MARK 16:6-7

Sorrow skews our sense of security in God, causing us to doubt Him. Even though Jesus promised His disciples He would come back to life after three days, they forgot. After Christ's gruesome death on the cross, His followers were filled with fear and sadness. He told them the truth of His resurrection, but the disciples' hearts had not caught up with their minds.

Like the disciples, I struggle with spiritual amnesia. I forget my heavenly Father has promised to heal my broken heart. I stew in sadness instead of receiving God's gladness. I let my emotions get the better of me when I feel alone and afraid, forgetful of His precious promise that He will never leave me or forsake me. I grow weary wondering if my physical needs will be met and my financial obligations covered. Yet I can rest, for my Savior does what He says He will do. He brings back to life what was dead for His good purposes.

❧

"Jesus answered them, 'Destroy this temple, and I will raise it again in three days'...But the temple he had spoken of was his body" (John 2:19-21).

Has sorrow over a loss led you to lose faith? Has worry trapped your mind? Do you wallow around in what-ifs? You can take Christ at His word, for He is 100 percent trustworthy in what He says and what He does. Life may not make sense at the moment, but give God time. Cloudy circumstances will give way to blue skies of hope. His promise

145

of grace and mercy is 24/7 in heaven. Your heavenly Father longs to love you through trials so your trust grows even sweeter.

As you experience the resurrected Christ in your life, not everyone will support you. Some will scoff at you, some will ignore you, and a few will rejoice with you. Regardless of someone's disbelief, hold fast to the truth that Jesus rose from the grave. By God's grace you can still rise above your circumstances as a testament to His wonder-working power in your life. Since Jesus rose from the grave, all who believe can rise from their grave of sin, sorrow, and death. God says so!

—⁂—

"We were therefore buried with him through baptism into death in order that, just as Christ was raised from the dead through the glory of the Father, we too may live a new life" (Romans 6:4).

Heavenly Father, I rest in Your promises and trust You to carry out Your purposes.

Related Readings
Acts 13:32-34; 1 Corinthians 15:3-8; 2 Corinthians 1:20; James 2:5

71

Thankful for the Ordinary

―――――― ∞ ――――――

When he was at the table with them, he took bread, gave
thanks, broke it and began to give it to them. Then
their eyes were opened and they recognized him.

LUKE 24:30-31

The eyes of Christ's two hosts were opened to His presence when
they saw His grateful heart. The Holy Spirit revealed the gift of
the Son through the expression of gratitude for God's gifts. Yes, we
grow in our likeness of Jesus when we thank God for the small things
in life. His rising sun brightens the tops of shaded trees with autumn's
yellow leaves. Light rain hums a fussy baby to sleep. Children can run,
skip, and laugh on a carpet of green grass. A blanket of snow calms the
soul. The ordinary blessings of God are extraordinary in their beauty.

Yes, we are compelled to give thanks to our heavenly Father for His
everyday provision. It may be the moment by moment opportunity
to fill our lungs with God's oxygen or the meals He routinely provides
to fill our stomachs. Ordinary, daily blessings from Jesus give us the
privilege to slow down and say thank you. Perhaps we are grateful for
a spouse's support, a child's love, a parent's laughter, or a friend's faith.
No one can have too much appreciation.

―――――― ∞ ――――――

"Bless the LORD, O my soul;
And all that is within me, bless His holy name!
Bless the LORD, O my soul,
And forget not all His benefits" (Psalm 103:1-2 NKJV).

How do you regularly express gratitude to God for your job? What
are some ways you can say thank you to your coworkers? Maybe a

simple "thank you" or a written note of appreciation. Offer to be responsible for a friend's tasks so they can take a day off. Show gratitude with a gift of cash, so an employee can take their spouse to dinner or pay down debt.

Be bold when you break bread to pray a sincere blessing of thanksgiving for the Lord's provision. Mix it up at mealtime and ask each person around the table to share one thing they are thankful to God for. Make a list of the Lord's blessings you can refer to when you have a bad day. Look for Christ's gifts in your ordinary, everyday life. Brag on Jesus to others who may need Him. Respectfully and humbly declare what good things God has given you to enjoy!

"Who forgives all your iniquities,
Who heals all your diseases,
Who redeems your life from
destruction" (Psalm 103:3-4 NKJV).

Heavenly Father, thank You for the incredible, ordinary gifts You give me every day.

Related Readings

Deuteronomy 8:3; Nehemiah 12:47; Psalm 68:19; Acts 2:42-47; Hebrews 3:13

72

Thankful for the Extraordinary

I thank You, Father, Lord of heaven and earth, that You have hidden these things from the wise and prudent and revealed them to babes.

LUKE 10:21 NKJV

Jesus was full of the Holy Spirit and full of joy over God's revelation of truth. His joy exploded in thanksgiving to His heavenly Father. The intellectually proud have no knowledge of the Holy One, but He is revealed to the humble in heart. Self-proclaimed sages cannot see what babies in the faith already understand—that Jesus Christ is the Son of God. Prophets and kings longed to see and hear from the Messiah, but the meek disciples were the first to experience their Savior Jesus.

Our heavenly Father is available to show Himself and reveal to us His will and His ways. What conceited scholars miss, we can receive through a humble and contrite heart. Our Lord chose us to champion His truth because our human credentials are very modest compared to the surpassing glory of our Savior Jesus Christ. The Holy Spirit reveals to us what we need to know for today's decisions. As a sovereign king has control over a country, the Spirit is sovereign over truth's revelation.

"He who forms the mountains,
who creates the wind,
and who reveals his thoughts to mankind,
who turns dawn to darkness,
and treads on the heights of the earth—
the Lord God Almighty is his name" (Amos 4:13).

Joy wells up in our hearts and explodes into thanksgiving when we recall the revelation of God. His Spirit convicted us of our need to repent of our sin and receive Christ and His love as the payment of our sin. We rejoice knowing our name is written in heaven. It is an extraordinary blessing to have the assurance of eternal life with the Lord and with all those who love Him.

How can you express gratitude to God for the forgiveness of your sins? What is some evidence of the joy of the Lord in your life? Praise and thanksgiving to the Almighty are fruits of your joyful heart. You thank Him when you see the smile on the face of a loved one humming hymns and tearing up at the reading of God's Word. Oh yes, the revelation of Jesus Christ is extraordinary to those with an eye on their eternal dwelling!

"For we know that if the earthly tent we live in is destroyed, we have a building from God, an eternal house in heaven, not built by human hands" (2 Corinthians 5:1).

Heavenly Father, thank You for the extraordinary revelation of Your Son Jesus Christ.

Related Readings
Daniel 2:22,28; John 1:18; 1 Corinthians 1:26-29; 1 Peter 1:10-12; Revelation 20:12

73

Introduction to Jesus

❦

You will go on before the Lord to prepare the way for him, to give his
people the knowledge of salvation through the forgiveness of their sins.

LUKE 1:76-77

Followers of Jesus have the unique opportunity and calling—like
John the Baptist—to introduce people to Jesus. Belief in the Lord
frees us from the bondage of sin and lifts away our sorrows. Yes, outside of the Savior, the soul is secluded and exiled from intimacy with
Almighty God. But there is a promised land of peace and forgiveness
that Christians can announce to the spiritually needy. An introduction
to Jesus opens beautiful vistas of faith.

Like Christ's faithful forerunner John, it is from the Spirit's fullness that we have moral authority and spiritual support to plant seeds
of hope in hurting hearts. Moreover, it's out of our humility and compassion that we confront injustice and remind offenders of God's call
to repentance. Seasons of suffering are an ideal time to talk of the ide-
als Christ came to live and die for.

❦

"Here is a trustworthy saying that deserves full
acceptance: Christ Jesus came into the world to save
sinners—of whom I am the worst" (1 Timothy 1:15).

Are you a follower of Jesus worth following? If not, perhaps now is
the time to join a support group, install pornographic protection soft-
ware, go to marriage counseling, or break off a relationship. In a word,
repent. Your ability to effectively introduce people to Jesus is only limited by your consistent life for Christ. Make sure the quality of your
character keeps up with the quantity of your spiritual conversations.

You know the cure for the terminal disease of sin. Your knowledge of salvation is not to be kept to yourself, but prayerfully shared with others. Having a spirit of gratitude and generosity compels us to share the gospel in the power of the Holy Spirit. Your part is to introduce seekers to Jesus—and your heavenly Father's part is to draw them to faith. Like a marriage matchmaker you receive great joy by introducing others to Christ!

"No one can come to me unless the Father
who sent me draws them" (John 6:44).

Heavenly Father, use me to introduce others to saving faith in Jesus.

Related Readings

Isaiah 40:3; Jeremiah 31:3; Luke 1:17; Acts 8:30-39

74

Thankful for Answered Prayer

Jesus looked up and said, "Father, I thank you that you have heard me. I knew that you always hear me."

JOHN 11:41-42

Jesus thanked His Father for answered prayer before His prayer was answered. His heart was so in tune with the heart of the Father that He could boldly ask knowing it was the will of God. In the same way, our Savior calls us to align our hearts with our heavenly Father's heart. His plan is for our desires to be His desires, our wants to be His wants, our goals to be His goals, and our wills to be His will. Prayer aligns our hearts with God's heart.

What prayers do you need to pray? What is Christ asking you to confidently pray in His name, knowing He will answer in the future? Perhaps it's a job promotion you can thank God for even before it happens. You can praise the Lord today for your wayward child, whom you have a peace in your heart will eventually come back to their Savior Jesus. Or you can pray with the Spirit's certainty over an uncertain illness that threatens your joy. Whatever you face, you can face it down with faith in your heavenly Father.

"You may ask me for anything in my
name, and I will do it" (John 14:14).

We pray in Jesus's name, hoping for Him to be glorified through answered prayer. When Jesus is lifted up, men and women are drawn to Him. We pray in Christ's name for believers to grow in their faith and for unbelievers to come to faith. Oh, the joy of seeing someone

153

come to know Jesus in personal salvation because they saw God transforming the life of a loved one. Gratitude glorifies God!

As we look to the Lord and thank Him for answered prayer, He may call us to be a part of His provision. Jesus told the disciples to pray to the Lord of the harvest for laborers, and as they prayed, He called them to labor for Him. So, what is your role in providing for God's people? Be grateful, for God has you positioned to be a part of His answered prayers!

———⌘———

"He said to them, 'The harvest truly is great, but the laborers are few; therefore pray the Lord of the harvest to send out laborers into His harvest'" (Luke 10:2 NKJV).

Heavenly Father, I praise You for the assurance of answered prayers in the future.

Related Readings

2 Kings 20:5; 2 Chronicles 7:15; Psalm 17:6; Matthew 7:7; 1 John 5:14-15

Authentic Fruit

⁓

I am the true vine, and my Father is the gardener. He cuts off
every branch in me that bears no fruit, while every branch that
does bear fruit he prunes so that it will be even more fruitful.

JOHN 15:1-2

There is authentic fruit, fake fruit, and the fruit of sin. Followers of
Jesus who are engrafted into Him, the true vine, flourish with the
fruit of the Spirit. It is beautiful to see and taste that the Lord is good.
Where there is love there will be joy, where there is joy there will be
peace, and where there is peace there will be forbearance. Imagine one
tree that bears a variety of fruit. In the same way, one life that abides
in Christ displays an array of character traits. The fruit of faith comes
in many varieties.

Authentic fruit grows in abundance, while fruit forced in the flesh
provides a meager return at the harvest. So, beware of fake fruit that is
the result of human discipline, natural skills, and temperament traits.
Like the plastic fruit that sits in a bowl on your grandmother's dining
room table, inauthentic fruit looks good but offers no life-giving nutrients. Fake fruit mimics the real image for a while, but when tasted, it
is exposed as a cheap imitation.

⁓

"You have planted wickedness,
you have reaped evil,
you have eaten the fruit of deception" (Hosea 10:13).

The fruit of sin looks appealing, but tastes bitter. Just as the serpent tempted Eve and Adam to partake of sin's fruit, Satan continues
to lure us to feast on his deceitful delicacies. We are wise not to plant

sin's seeds or cultivate its influence. If iniquity begins to bloom, it must be purged and destroyed by the Spirit's shears of conviction. We must confess and repent. Lives purged of sin make room for authentic fruit to flourish in a harvest of holiness.

Furthermore, invite your heavenly Father to inspect your fruit. Will He discover the fruit of the Spirit, self, or sin? Motives need a constant cleansing to ensure you are led by the Spirit and not driven by the flesh. Prayerful persuasion replaces impatient manipulation. Bearing authentic fruit is a lifetime process, as we seek to replace the unrighteous with the righteous. Saved souls and Christlike character are authentic fruits that glorify God.

"[May you be] filled with the fruit of righteousness
that comes through Jesus Christ—to the glory
and praise of God" (Philippians 1:11).

Heavenly Father, I surrender to You. Please examine the fruit in my life, making sure that it is authentic.

Related Readings
Matthew 21:43; Luke 3:8-9; 22:18; Romans 7:4; Colossians 1:6

Fan or Follower

*Whoever serves me must follow me; and where I am, my servant
also will be. My Father will honor the one who serves me.*

JOHN 12:26

Fans of Jesus stay a safe distance from Him, only observing from
the outside, but followers of Jesus are active servants for Him. Fans
have fun at a Christian concert, but they go on living for this life. Followers have fun at a Christian concert, but they go on living for the life
to come. Fans obsess over anxious thoughts: "What if I lose my job?
What if I lose my health? What if I lose my house?" Followers rest in
being with Jesus. They remain faithful when the Lord calls them to
serve. They follow by faith.

A fan of Jesus is emotionally whiplashed by life's ups and downs.
Their joy and peace waver, like the peaks and valleys of a stock market
pricing chart. They may be double-minded or unstable in their faith
commitment. If things go well, they are well. If things go bad, they are
bad. Their spiritual voice grows hoarse cheering on other Christ followers who sacrifice all, but they don't plan to give up very much for
God. Fans are comfortable as spectators not servants.

<ⵌ>

"If you care for your orchard, you'll enjoy its fruit;
if you honor your boss, you'll be
honored" (Proverbs 27:18 MSG).

As a follower of Jesus, you see Him as your Savior and Master. You
don't passively watch Him work. Rather, you actively roll up your
sleeves and serve with Him as the Spirit leads. Beautifully and generously, the Lord invites you to enjoy the fruit of your labor. Years of

sowing biblical teaching into the heart of your child will grow a harvest of humility, love, and laughter. When you give something up for God, you get it back bountifully from God.

Your heavenly Father honors you when you follow and serve Him. Your fidelity is not mist on a mirror that quickly melts away. Instead, your faith is the continual flow of living water from your heart, and it bubbles out of your love relationship with the Lord. Your heavenly Father honors those who honor Him with His abundant grace. He owns you because He bought you with the blood of His Son Jesus. The One who gave His all deserves your all!

"They will wage war against the Lamb, but the Lamb will triumph over them because he is Lord of lords and King of kings—and with him will be his called, chosen and faithful followers" (Revelation 17:14).

Heavenly Father, my heart's desire is to be an engaged follower of Yours who serves where You want me to serve.

Related Readings
Matthew 10:39; Mark 8:35; Luke 19:12-27; John 17:24;
      Colossians 3:1-2

77

Strategic Simplicity

⎯⎯⎯⎯⎯⎯⎯⎯ ⚬⚬⚬ ⎯⎯⎯⎯⎯⎯⎯⎯

*Freely you have received; freely give. Do not get any gold
or silver or copper to take with you in your belts—no bag
for the journey or extra shirt or sandals or a staff.*

MATTHEW 10:8-10

Jesus gives His disciples simple instructions with a simple strategy: Share the gospel, heal the sick, and cast out demons. The Lord encouraged an unencumbered life so His followers would be free to focus on eternal life. Christ keeps it simple because He knows we are easily distracted. It is easy to drift into complex schemes that drain the life out of opportunities to give life. The gospel needs to be communicated clearly, as the Spirit's power uses this earnest simplicity.

Status, stuff, society, sin, and self all complicate life. Such things aren't necessary in the kingdom of God. Like an intricate spiderweb, the complexity of life can trap us. If we are tied up, we will be unable to respond in spontaneous service. The motto of earnest simplicity is "less is more." Because God has freely given to us, we are free to freely give to others. Avoid sin's complexity so you are available to bless others with pure joy.

⎯⎯⎯⎯⎯ ⚬⚬⚬ ⎯⎯⎯⎯⎯

"Evildoers are snared by their own sin,
but the righteous shout for joy and
are glad" (Proverbs 29:6).

Earnest simplicity does not mean we are all called to live a monastic life, but it does mean we are free from the seduction of stuff. An unencumbered life is not isolated from society, but it is free from culture's control. A life with margin does not seek status, but it does use success as a platform to care for the unfortunate in Jesus's name. Enjoy your season of simplicity. Let the Son's love shine through your soul. Simplicity points to your Savior!

Perhaps it's time to resign a role or responsibility that no longer requires your attention. Doing so will make you available for impromptu interactions with hurting hearts. Sometimes spur-of-the-moment ministry opportunities at your church mean the most. Be on call for Christ and He will open doors for you to share the gospel with lost souls. Create margin with money, so in the moment you can freely give to those hungry for help. Keep it simple so the Spirit can work through you!

———❧———

"Strip down, start running—and never quit! No
extra spiritual fat, no parasitic sins. Keep your
eyes on Jesus, who both began and finished
this race we're in" (Hebrews 12:2-3 MSG).

Heavenly Father, may I speak the gospel and simply live by faith in You.

Related Readings
Proverbs 15:16-19; 1 Corinthians 2:1-5; Hebrews 11:13-16; 1 Peter 1:17

Jesus Is God

―――――∞――――――

*Anyone who has seen me has seen the Father. How can
you say, "Show us the Father"? Don't you believe that I
am in the Father, and that the Father is in me?*

JOHN 14:9-10

Jesus Christ is God. He claimed oneness with His heavenly Father
to His disciples. When they saw Jesus, they saw the Father. He dis-
played His divinity with His perfect character. He validated His status as Savior and Lord by His miracles. His clear public teaching of
His equality with God brought out the wrath of the religious leaders. His elevation to deity in the minds of mere mortals was a threat to
the reigning monarchs of men. Christ is in God, and God is in Christ.

Philip struggled to believe in Jesus as God. He wanted to see before
he believed, but His Savior bid him to believe *before* seeing. Philip had
been around the Lord and His works, but the Lord had not done a
personal work of grace in his heart. Has your faith become so familiar
that it is only a family tradition? Has Christ really captured your heart?
Trust in Jesus as God transforms your life!

――――∞――――

"Just as you received Christ Jesus as Lord,
continue to live your lives in him, rooted
and built up in him" (Colossians 2:6-7).

Since Jesus is in the Father and the Father in Jesus, by faith we are
in Christ and Christ is in us. This is a mystery of the Christian life: that
the fullness of God lives within all who embrace Jesus as God. When
we said "I do" to our Savior, we vowed that He was everything He
claimed to be. Our groom, Christ, desires us to grow in grace each day

through oneness with Him. Christ in us transforms us into His loving likeness.

Therefore, when people see you, do they see Jesus? Is your soul so surrendered to your Savior that what comes from your inner being is beautiful to behold? A soul submitted to Christ loves like Christ. A mind saturated with the thoughts of Christ thinks like Christ. A heart filled with the character of Christ behaves like Christ. A life aligned with the Lord is one with His will. We believe and then we are able to see. Our next step of trust in Jesus shows us more of Him!

"In order that they may know the mystery of God, namely, Christ, in whom are hidden all the treasures of wisdom and knowledge" (Colossians 2:2-3).

Heavenly Father, I believe Christ is in me and I am in Christ. By grace through faith may He live His life through me.

Related Readings
Isaiah 9:6; 2 Corinthians 4:4; Philippians 2:6; Colossians 1:15; Hebrews 1:3

79

Affection and Acceptance

⸻⸺⸻

Then people brought little children to Jesus for him to place his hands on them and pray for them. But the disciples rebuked them. Jesus said, "Let the little children come to me, and do not hinder them, for the kingdom of heaven belongs to such as these."

MATTHEW 19:13-14

Jesus was tender and tough. He took the time to love little children, but He was also bold to confront greed in the face of businessmen using God for personal gain. However, most of the time Jesus modeled affection toward others—and acceptance toward those who had experienced rejection. He graciously extended both.

Do you daily receive the affection and acceptance of Almighty God? Have you begun to comprehend the depth and breadth of His magnificent love? What a Savior and lover of your soul! A close friend may give you the cold shoulder, but Jesus warmly embraces your cares and concerns. Perhaps a fellow Christian rejected you for your indiscretions, but Jesus accepts you despite your failures and lifts you up to walk faithfully with Him.

⸺⸻⸺

"Jesus straightened up and asked her, 'Woman, where are they? Has no one condemned you?' 'No one, sir,' she said. 'Then neither do I condemn you,' Jesus declared. 'Go now and leave your life of sin'" (John 8:10-11).

Acceptance is a magnet for those who feel isolated and misunderstood. Your spouse can get caught up in their own concerns, which can harm your relationship's intimacy. It's when you feel this relational distance that you turn to Christ and enjoy His closeness. Only Jesus provides acceptance all the time. Affection is a tender touch, an empathetic ear, a compassionate conversation, and a patient prayer. It looks beyond the ugliness of sin and the harshness of humanity—and engages the heart. Affection is not concerned about getting, but is consumed by giving.

Who in your life needs your affection and acceptance? Does your child feel your support? Do you honor your distant parents with love and respect? What about friends and family who are consumed with their own concerns—do you invite them into your life to experience your family's joy and the compassion of Christ? Reach out to those whom others have rejected and watch the Lord do a work of redeeming love.

"Very truly I tell you, whoever accepts anyone I send accepts me; and whoever accepts me accepts the one who sent me" (John 13:20).

How does Christ accept me and show His affection? Whom can I serve in the same way?

Related Readings

Deuteronomy 10:15; Acts 15:8; Romans 14:1-3; Philippians 1:8

80

Silver and Gold

⸺◦◦⸺

On coming to the house, they saw the child with his mother Mary,
and they bowed down and worshiped him. Then they opened their
treasures and presented him with gifts of gold, frankincense and myrrh.

MATTHEW 2:11

The Magi came with genuine gifts of gold, frankincense, and myrrh for the newborn Messiah. However, this was the closest Christ would come to obtaining treasures for Himself. He arrived in the world with no economic mandate or political agenda. His goal was not to bring finances to bear as a solution to poverty or the nation's war-torn conditions. No, Jesus was born to bring the new birth of a prosperous soul, a peaceful mind, and a forgiven heart. Gold was not His goal.

We have to honestly ask ourselves, is our plan to fix the culture with financial solutions, or is the Spirit's transforming power our remedy? What is our role in bringing the life-giving gospel of Jesus to the spiritually bankrupt? Jesus lost what was rightfully His, so He could reach the lost. He came to seek and to save the lost so they might be saved from sin, self, and Satan. A global movement of God does not depend on money, but on our hearts being moved by God.

⸺◦◦⸺

"A good name is more desirable than great riches;
to be esteemed is better than silver
or gold" (Proverbs 22:1).

History describes a powerful church when it wasn't prosperous and a powerless church when it was prosperous. Thus, we go back to the beginning of the Christian faith, where Jesus lay in a modest manger. We rely on God, not gold or government. We worship the One whose kingdom is not of this world—the One who reigns over the hearts of humans. Yes, your good name is more valuable than great riches. Use your influence to influence others to trust Jesus.

Some think they need more stuff, but what they need is to be loved by their Lord. Your material means may be modest, but your spiritual resources are abundant. Stay focused on a faithful expression of love and prayer, and don't get caught up in the influence of money and materialism. Like the early Christians, you may not have silver and gold, but you have God and He has you.

"Peter said, 'Silver or gold I do not have, but
what I do have I give you. In the name of Jesus
Christ of Nazareth, walk'" (Acts 3:6).

Heavenly Father, help me lean into Your power and not depend on money to solve spiritual issues.

Related Readings

Proverbs 3:3-4; Ezekiel 34:16; Luke 19:10; John 8:58;
    Revelation 9:20

81

Recognize and Receive

⸎

*Though the world was made through him, the world
did not recognize him. He came to that which was
his own, but his own did not receive him.*

JOHN 1:9-11

God stationed a star over Bethlehem to celebrate the birth of His Son Jesus, the true light of the world. The bright light over Bethlehem became a beacon of hope for all who believed. But Christ—the Creator and owner of the world—is shunned by the majority of its inhabitants. Jesus was born to light up our sin-darkened world with His illuminating love, though many will never accept Him.

How can so great a love go unrecognized? How can people around the globe or down the street fail to see their Lord? Put simply, some love darkness more than the light. They believe their deeds, done in the darkness, are somehow hidden from God's sight. But He reveals everything and calls us to repent. This is why Spirit-filled Christians make our culture uncomfortable. Jesus invites us to walk in the light as He is in the light. Light exposes darkness.

⸎

"When Jesus spoke again to the people, he
said, 'I am the light of the world. Whoever
follows me will never walk in darkness, but
will have the light of life'" (John 8:12).

Jesus was rejected by His own. He came to heal the sick, but those with a sick soul failed to receive Him as their remedy for unrighteousness. He came to preach good tidings, but His fellow citizens assumed He was just another prophet. Jesus was rejected by those who should have known better, and He was received by those who didn't know any better but to believe God sent His Son into the world to save them from their sins.

What happens once we recognize that Jesus is the light of the world? Almighty God expects us by faith to receive Christ into our lives as our Savior and Lord. We embrace the light of His love, and we walk away from our shameful ways done in the darkness. When we receive Jesus, we are purified by His blood. We walk with Him in the light, and we enjoy His forever fellowship with each other!

———⁓⁓⁓———

"But if we walk in the light, as he is in the light, we have fellowship with one another, and the blood of Jesus, his Son, purifies us from all sin" (1 John 1:7).

Heavenly Father, lead me to follow You, the true light of my life, and to receive Jesus as my Lord and Savior.

Related Readings

Isaiah 49:6; 53:3; Romans 13:12; Ephesians 5:8; 1 Thessalonians 5:5

82

Abundant Forgiveness

*"Lord, how many times shall I forgive my brother or sister
who sins against me? Up to seven times?"
Jesus answered, "I tell you, not seven times
but seventy-seven times."*

MATTHEW 18:21-22

Sin's offense hurts. There is no doubt about it. Sin wounds indiscriminately. It is no respecter of persons. Sin builds walls. It ravishes relationships and it separates. Sin is a sorry excuse for wrong behavior. Just the sound of the word solicits negative emotion. Sin is deceptive, carnal, and Christ-less. Sin is unfair, sad, and sometimes sadistic.

Sin follows a process of desire, conception, birth, maturity, and death. James describes its diabolical development: "Then, after desire has conceived, it gives birth to sin; and sin, when it is full-grown, gives birth to death" (James 1:15). So sin is not to be taken lightly. It can inflict pain and kill relationships.

When someone's sin crushes your dreams, you are to forgive them. When someone's sin steals from you, you are to forgive them. This level of forgiveness is counterintuitive and countercultural, but it is the way of Christ. Forgiveness is God's game plan. You will lose if you don't forgive. Withholding forgiveness will torture your soul. It is unhealthy for the body and emotions.

"[Love] keeps no record of wrongs" (1 Corinthians 13:5).

True forgiveness comes from the heart of the one offended. It is not a flippant acknowledgment, but a sincere removal of anything that is owed. When the offended one forgives, he or she no longer expects an apology, a payback, or a change. Forgiveness is letting go of the hurt, anger, and shame. When you forgive you are free. When you forgive you trust God to judge others in His time. His judgment is just. God can be trusted with the consequences of sin's offense.

Ultimately, you continue to forgive others because your heavenly Father continues to forgive you. Jesus does not have forgiveness quotas. The forgiveness of the cross was swift, full, final, and forever. Unlock your relational restraints with the key of forgiveness. Write a letter with tear-soaked ink outlining your forgiveness. Call or email someone today and let them know that because you are forgiven, you forgive them. Set others free with forgiveness, and you set yourself free. There is freedom in Christ. Forgive fast—and forgive often.

———

"Jesus said, 'Father, forgive them, for they do
not know what they are doing'" (Luke 23:34).

Who by God's grace do I need to forgive? Have I accepted Christ's forgiveness?

Related Readings

Genesis 50:17; Psalm 130:4; Luke 17:3; Ephesians 4:32

83

A Word from God

No word from God will ever fail.

LUKE 1:37

Because of the Spirit's inspiration, God's word is always successful. Mary and Elizabeth received a word from the Lord that He had blessed them with very special children—sons who would represent their heavenly Father with servant spirits and who would boldly proclaim the word of God. The Bible communicates Christ's words in a transformational way.

Do you read the Bible for information or inspiration? Is your goal to study the Word, learn facts about God, or to know God? If you are a serious student of Scripture, you will encounter Christ in your search for truth. The Word of God is a hammer that chisels pride from your heart, a fire that brands truth into your brain, and a sword that slices ego from your soul. Watch out for a word from God, for it will lead you to success.

"'Is not my word like fire,' declares the
LORD, 'and like a hammer that breaks a
rock in pieces?'" (Jeremiah 23:29).

Moreover, as you take time to meditate on God's Word, your mind will marinate in wise thinking. Beyond your personal prayer and study, make sure you are engaged with a small group of Christ followers who will challenge and sharpen your thinking. Changes come from a clear understanding of why you believe what you believe. Ask your heavenly Father to fill your mind with what really matters to Him.

Do you have a word from God for a major decision you are facing?

If not, wait until you do. Then validate your thinking with other godly advisors. If you do, then proceed in the power of the Holy Spirit and trust the Lord with the results. It may not make sense in the short term, but you can trust Him in the long run. God's word always wins out!

———∞∞∞———

"The word of God is alive and active. Sharper than any double-edged sword, it penetrates even to dividing soul and spirit, joints and marrow; it judges the thoughts and attitudes of the heart" (Hebrews 4:12).

Heavenly Father, write Your Word on my heart so I grow to know You better.

Related Readings

Luke 11:28; Acts 12:24; 1 Thessalonians 2:13; 2 Timothy 2:9

84

Modest Means

⎯⎯⎯⎯⎯⎯⎯⎯⎯∽∾⎯⎯⎯⎯⎯⎯⎯⎯⎯

She gave birth to her firstborn, a son. She wrapped
him in cloths and placed him in a manger, because
there was no guest room available for them.

LUKE 2:7

J esus came into the world in a modest manger with parents who had modest means. Mary and Joseph were long on love but short on financial resources. But in God's economy, a family first needs faith in their Provider and not in the provision. A family who prays together has a higher probability of staying together. A home rich in relationships experiences true joy. Modest financial means can liberate one's love for the Lord.

You may receive a cool reception from those who feel superior because of their self-proclaimed social status. Some look down on the work of your hands, for their hands have not been soiled by sweat and physical labor. A smug countenance is a sign of pride, while humility shows on a kind and compassionate face. Indeed, modesty makes room for humility.

⎯⎯⎯⎯∽∾⎯⎯⎯⎯

"I also want you to think about how this keeps
your significance from getting blown up into
self-importance. For no matter how significant
you are, it is only because of what you are
a part of" (1 Corinthians 12:19 MSG).

Are you a little embarrassed that you don't have the cutest clothes, the coolest car, or the most decorated home? Don't let the "comparison trap" steal your trust in God's game plan and His good things. You may seem ordinary by the world's standards, but your life—when surrendered to your Savior—has extraordinary potential. Give Him all you have.

Maybe you are newly married or you know a newlywed couple. This modest season is a great time to learn contentment in Christ and how to serve Him and others unselfishly. Give your modest means over to the Lord, and He will multiply it for His glory. He redeems your limited time with creative opportunities, and He stretches your humble finances beyond a strict budget. He even makes your rich relationships richer. Dedicate your modest means to your Master Jesus. Like a soft rain, He will refresh dry hearts.

—∞—

"Whoever can be trusted with very little can
also be trusted with much" (Luke 16:10).

Heavenly Father, take my modest means and multiply them for Your glory.

Related Readings
Exodus 16:17; Proverbs 16:8; Luke 19:17; 1 Corinthians 12:23

85

God with Us

All this took place to fulfill what the Lord had said through the prophet: "The virgin will conceive and give birth to a son, and they will call him Immanuel" (which means "God with us").

MATTHEW 1:22-23

Wow! The Creator came to dwell with His creation. The all-knowing One came to teach teachers and students limited by their lack of knowledge and understanding. The ever-present One came to comfort hurting people who were stuck in their suffering. The all-powerful One came to serve weak people, empowering them with His Spirit. The Almighty sent His only Son Jesus into the world, fully God and fully man. Yes, the Word became flesh!

God is with us to face down our fears. God is with us in our doubts. God is with us in our hurts, applying His healing balm of grace. God is with us in our transitions. God is with us at work and home. God is with us in our uncertainty. God is with us when we feel His presence and when we don't feel Him near. God is with us in our successes and in our failures. God is with us, for us, for His glory!

"Surely I am with you always, to the very
end of the age" (Matthew 28:20).

God is with us in our modern technology and our old-fashioned activities. The Lord is with us in our big cities and our small towns. Jesus is with us when we feel joy, laughter, and loss. Christ is with us, comforting us in our pain and encouraging us to persevere for Him. He is with us in the ups and the downs. He is with us, in us, and working through us!

Therefore, because Christ is with you, you can be confident of His wisdom and direction. Fools flounder for lack of faith, but you have the Faithful One as the facilitator of your circumstances. Your Savior Jesus has saved you from your sins, and He commands you to follow His ways and experience His life. He gave His life and came back to life for you!

"The LORD himself will give you a sign: The
virgin will conceive and give birth to a son,
and will call him Immanuel" (Isaiah 7:14).

Heavenly Father, thank You for being with us on earth and for being in my life.

Related Readings

1 Kings 8:57; Psalm 46:11; Isaiah 8:10; Acts 10:41; Ephesians 2:6

86

Love Listens

⟋⟋⟋

*A cloud appeared and covered them, and a voice came from
the cloud: "This is my Son, whom I love. Listen to him!"*

MARK 9:7

A heart full of love listens first to the Lord. A humble heart remembers that God created two ears and one mouth for a reason. The tongue untempered by love is a prime target for the tempter—Satan himself. However, love longs to listen and understand what Christ says before making conversation. Words incubated in a heart of love have a positive effect on hearers. Love listens to Jesus before jumping to judgment.

We need the words of our heavenly Father to work out our wrong thinking—*before* we share potentially abrasive words. For example, we pause during family conflict to contemplate Christ's teaching to be peacemakers. We become a voice of reason and patience when angry words have broken trust and erased respect. We listen to both sides and then offer solutions based on forgiveness and an ongoing process of godly counsel.

⟋⟋⟋

"To you who are listening I say: Love your enemies,
do good to those who hate you" (Luke 6:27).

When God is in your heart, you listen to others even when you don't feel you are being heard. Your patient love does not have to make its point, because listening to and understanding the other person's viewpoint is more important. As you lovingly listen, you learn—from friends and enemies alike. Your quieted spirit becomes a student, ready to learn from anyone. Perhaps you learn kindness from a cashier or acceptance from a greeter. Love listens and learns.

Love is slow to speak and quick to listen. It doesn't seek to impress people with its smart and clever speech. Instead, it carries a conversation with emotional comfort and caring words. You are most comfortable in your own skin when your goal is to first listen to the Lord and then His precious children. Lovingly listen, and some will invite your influence into their life. Consecrate your conversations to Christ and He will speak.

———⊶⊷———

"In these last days he has spoken to us by his Son, whom he appointed heir of all things, and through whom also he made the universe" (Hebrews 1:2).

Heavenly Father, use me to lovingly listen to You and Your children.

Related Readings

Deuteronomy 30:20; Proverbs 10:19; Isaiah 55:3; James 1:19; 2:5

87

Finding God

⎯⎯⎯❦⎯⎯⎯

*Jesus said to him, "Today salvation has come to this
house, because this man, too, is a son of Abraham. For
the Son of Man came to seek and to save the lost."*

LUKE 19:9-10

A Christ-less human condition is lost and in need of a Savior. An
unsaved soul is in search of peace, forgiveness, and eternal life in
heaven. A soul in search of wholeness may take detours into the plea-
sures of sin for a season, but when awakened, it comes back to the narrow road, looking for the Lord. Faith is found in a humble and sincere
search for God.

⎯⎯⎯❦⎯⎯⎯

"Enter through the narrow gate. For wide is
the gate and broad is the road that leads to
destruction, and many enter through it. But small
is the gate and narrow the road that leads to
life, and only a few find it" (Matthew 7:13-14).

Finding God is educational since the Bible contains 66 textbooks
in the University of Truth. Jesus is the main character of the story, ever
looking to give glory to His heavenly Father. He is truth personified,
and His promise is the only way to God. Faith in Jesus as the Son of
God is the bridge from an endless hell to eternal salvation in heaven.

⎯⎯⎯❦⎯⎯⎯

"Thomas said to him, 'Lord, we don't know
where you are going, so how can we know
the way?' Jesus answered, 'I am the way and

> the truth and the life. No one comes to the
> Father except through me'" (John 14:5-6).

Not only does our inner being initiate an audience with Almighty God, but also His great love is out to get us. Righteousness out-romances the soul from sin. Listen for the Lord, and you will hear His tender calling for you to come home. But if you listen to sin, it will lead to sorrow. Listen, learn, and come to Christ in faith.

Look for the Lord by faith and you will find Him. Submit to the seducing and convicting power of the Holy Spirit in your heart. No one has ever regretted receiving the Lord Christ into their life, but many have wished they had not waited so long. A joyful, heavenly party awaits the ones who come to their senses and go home to their Savior Jesus!

> "'My son,' the father said, 'you are always with me, and
> everything I have is yours. But we had to celebrate and
> be glad, because this brother of yours was dead and is
> alive again; he was lost and is found'" (Luke 15:31-32).

Am I sincerely searching for God in worship, Bible study, prayer, and obedience?

Related Readings
Deuteronomy 4:29; Job 8:4-6; Acts 17:27; Hebrews 11:6

88

Alive and Well

―――――――∞∞∞―――――――

Later Jesus appeared to the Eleven as they were eating; he
rebuked them for their lack of faith and their stubborn refusal
to believe those who had seen him after he had risen.

MARK 16:14

Jesus Christ is alive and well. His earlier followers, taken aback by His death, initially denied His resurrection. They rejected reliable testimonies and refused to receive the truth of Christ's miracle. However, when they encountered the risen Lord, He rebuked them and then loved them. Unbelievers can loathe the Lord. Deists can deny Christ's deity. Agnostics can be apathetic over His resurrection, but He is alive and well.

Contemporary Christ-less cultures couldn't care less about Christ's resurrection, but it does not lessen His lordship over them. Everyone will one day confront Christ. "At the name of Jesus every knee should bow, in heaven and on earth and under the earth, and every tongue acknowledge that Jesus Christ is Lord" (Philippians 2:10-11). Easter is the grandest stage for Jesus followers to celebrate His resurrection and His relevance.

The Lord is alive and well in your heart. His resurrection resulted in Christ taking up residence in your soul and transforming your life. By faith you believed, and God gave you grace upon grace. Because He has risen from the grave, He has given all who confess Him as Lord abundant grace on earth and the promise of heaven with Him.

―――――∞∞∞―――――

"For if, by the trespass of the one man, death
reigned through that one man, how much more .
will those who receive God's abundant provision of

grace and of the gift of righteousness reign in life
through the one man, Jesus Christ" (Romans 5:17).

You can live large for the Lord because He has triumphed over sin, sorrow, death, and hell. Easter is your eternal encouragement that He is alive and well. There will always be doubters, but do not dwell in doubt. Focus on the undeniable force of faith that has captured you and millions before you. Because He has risen, you can rise above your circumstances, your hurt, and your fears.

—⊗⊗⊗—

"With great power the apostles continued to testify to
the resurrection of the Lord Jesus. And God's grace
was so powerfully at work in them all" (Acts 4:33).

Am I a disciple who ignores His power or one who proclaims His power?

Related Readings

Numbers 14:11; Matthew 28:17; Acts 10:41; 1 Corinthians 15:1-58

89

Hot-Hearted for God

*I know your deeds, that you are neither cold nor
hot. I wish you were either one or the other!*

REVELATION 3:15

As a young dad, I couldn't wait to bring my wife and our first new-born home from the hospital. Damp, dreary, and chilly outside, I built a roaring fire in our new Ashley wood-burning stove to assure our 1200-square-foot ranch home was warm and toasty. Our precious baby girl's little pink fingers and toes never felt a tinge of coolness because I kept feeding the fire with dried logs from a cord of wood just outside the back door. Like a hot fire, a hot heart for God needs its faith fueled.

The Lord looks displeasingly on a lukewarm life or on the institutional church that has lost its fiery faith for Christ. In the book of Revelation, Jesus calls out the church for blending in with the world. He would rather the church be totally dead and cold than a spiritual zombie, acting as if it were alive. Death knows it's dead, but being alive and going through the motions is deadly. God's great desire is for His bride the church and each disciple to burn brightly for the faith.

"You are the light of [Christ to] the world. A city set
on a hill cannot be hidden" (Matthew 5:14 AMP).

What does it mean to be a lukewarm Christian? One bit of evidence is that we use faith to further our self-serving agenda. When politicians use faith to get elected but do not back up their beliefs with their behavior, they are lukewarm. When businesspeople attend church to be seen and use their influence to acquire customers, but their life lacks integrity, they are lukewarm. When students say they are saved but then blend in with the crowd, they are lukewarm. When families smile at church but experience hell at home, they are lukewarm. Lukewarm is dishonesty.

Because the Lord loves us, He rebukes and disciplines us in our lukewarm condition. Christ calls us to be zealous in our faith—a zeal based on the knowledge of His Word and knowing Him. As our Lord says—repentance is the remedy for being lukewarm. Turn from our cold, dead past—let go of our lukewarm present and fuel our faith with loving obedience to God. The flue of our faith is opened when we kneel in prayer and offer praise to our Savior Jesus. Hot hearts ever glow for God.

———— ⚬⚬⚬ ————

"Where your treasure is, there your heart [your wishes, your desires; that on which your life centers] will be also" (Matthew 6:21 AMP).

What area of my life is lukewarm, in need of repentance and loving obedience?

Related Readings
1 Kings 8:61; Psalm 24:3-5; Jeremiah 15:16; 24:7; John 5:42

90

Seeing the Face of Jesus

*The throne of God and of the Lamb will be in the
city, and his servants will serve him. They will see his
face, and his name will be on their foreheads.*

REVELATION 22:3-4

In the South we like to say, "Good to see you." It's beyond a friendly greeting because it's much better to look into someone's eyes—see their soul and feel their heart. Even technology allows us to FaceTime so we might better see a friendly face and bridge the geographic chasm between us. Face-to-face interactions strengthen trust, deepen intimacy, influence decisions, and increase understanding of one another. Face-to-face encounters are "God moments" to reflect a face of faith, hope, comfort, and love. Face time is faith time.

Because we are earthbound, we cannot exactly see Christ's face. We enjoy glimpses of His glory in rapturous worship and intimate prayer. We see the outline of His countenance in the unselfish service of one of His choice servants, who quietly gives expecting nothing but praise to God in return. John gives us a Holy Spirit–inspired description of our eventual return to Eden, restored to its original purity and perfection. The face of Jesus lights up the eternal city with His illuminating love!

> "Anyone who has seen me has seen
> the Father" (John 14:9).

When Jesus looks compassionately on the woman caught in adultery, we see the mercy and holiness of our heavenly Father. He forgives but expects us not to sin. When Jesus angrily confronts the commercialism of God's place of worship, He addresses injustice and validates

His authority by predicting His coming resurrection. When Jesus hangs on the cross—He forgives ignorant men and comforts His grieving mom.

We seek His face in Scripture, and He fills our mind with truth and understanding. We seek His face in praise and worship, and He fills our heart with hope, gratitude, and glory to God. We seek His face in quiet contemplation, and He fills our souls with forgiveness, peace, and comfort. Death is only a maître d' who leads us to dine with the Lamb. The Man of Sorrows gently wipes away our tears. The faithful face of Jesus reflects no shame. It overflows with felicity while all eyes are captivated by Love.

"The eyes of the Lord are on those who fear him,
on those whose hope is in his
unfailing love" (Psalm 33:18).

Dear Jesus, I long to see You face-to-face. In the meantime, I seek Your face of love.

Related Readings

Genesis 32:30; Exodus 33:11; Matthew 5:8; John 6:46;
     1 Corinthians 13:12

How to Become a Disciple
of Jesus Christ

*Then Jesus came to them and said, "All authority in heaven
and on earth has been given to me. Therefore go and make
disciples of all nations, baptizing them in the name of the
Father and of the Son and of the Holy Spirit, and teaching
them to obey everything I have commanded you. And
surely I am with you always, to the very end of the age."*

MATTHEW 28:18-20

oly Scripture teaches us how to become disciples and how to
make disciples.

Believe

Belief in Jesus Christ as your Savior and Lord gives you eternal life
in heaven.

> If you declare with your mouth, "Jesus is Lord," and
> believe in your heart that God raised him from the dead,
> you will be saved (Romans 10:9).

Repent and Be Baptized

To repent is to turn from your sin and then publicly confess Christ
in baptism.

> Repent and be baptized, every one of you, in the name of
> Jesus Christ for the forgiveness of your sins. And you will
> receive the gift of the Holy Spirit (Acts 2:38).

Obey

Obedience is an indicator of our love for the Lord Jesus and His
presence in our life.

> Jesus replied, "Anyone who loves me will obey my teach-
> ing. My Father will love them, and we will come to them
> and make our home with them" (John 14:23).

Worship, Prayer, Community, Evangelism, and Study

Worship and prayer express our gratitude and honor to God and our dependence on His grace. Community and evangelism show our accountability to Christians and compassion for non-Christians. We study to apply the knowledge, understanding, and wisdom of God.

> Every day they continued to meet together in the temple courts. They broke bread in their homes and ate together with glad and sincere hearts, praising God and enjoying the favor of all the people. And the Lord added to their number daily those who were being saved (Acts 2:46-47).

Love God

Intimacy with Almighty God is a growing and loving relationship. We are loved by Him, so we can love others and be empowered by the Holy Spirit to obey His commands.

> Jesus replied: "'Love the Lord your God with all your heart and with all your soul and with all your mind.' This is the first and greatest commandment" (Matthew 22:37-38).

Love People

Our love for others flows from our love for our heavenly Father. We are able to love because He first loved us.

> And the second is like it: "Love your neighbor as yourself" (Matthew 22:39).

Make Disciples

We disciple others because we are grateful to God and to those who disciple us, and we want to obey Christ's last instructions before going to heaven.

> The things you have heard me say in the presence of many witnesses entrust to reliable people who will also be qualified to teach others (2 Timothy 2:2).

About the Author

Boyd Bailey is the president of the National Christian Foundation (NCF) Georgia. His passion is to encourage followers of Jesus to grow in their faith by being generous givers with their time, money, resources, and relationships.

Since 2004, Boyd has also served as president and founder of Wisdom Hunters, a ministry that connects people to Christ through devotional writing, with more than 100,000 daily email readers.

In 1999 Boyd cofounded Ministry Ventures, which has trained approximately 1000 faith-based nonprofits and coached for certification more than 200 ministries in the best practices of prayer, board development, ministry model, administration, and fundraising. By God's grace, these ministries have raised more than $100 million, and thousands of people have been led into growing relationships with Jesus Christ.

Prior to Ministry Ventures, Boyd was the national director for Crown Financial Ministries. He was instrumental in the expansion of Crown into 30 major markets across the United States. He was a key facilitator in the $25 million merger between Christian Financial Concepts and Crown Ministries.

Before his work with Crown, Boyd and Andy Stanley started First Baptist Atlanta's north campus, and as an elder, Boyd assisted Andy in the start of North Point Community Church.

Boyd received a bachelor of arts from Jacksonville State University and a master's of divinity from Southwestern Seminary in Fort Worth, Texas. Boyd and his wife, Rita, live in Roswell, Georgia. They have been married 34 years and are blessed with four daughters, three sons-in-law, and five grandchildren.

Wisdom Hunters

"He who walks with the wise grows wise, but a companion of fools suffers harm" (Proverbs 13:20).

In 2004, Boyd Bailey began to informally email personal reflections from his morning devotional time to a select group of fellow wisdom hunters. Over time, these informal emails grew into Wisdom Hunters Daily Devotional. Today, thanks to our friends at Family Christian Stores, these emails reach more than 100,000 wisdom hunters each morning.

We remain relentless in the pursuit of wisdom and continue to daily write raw, original, real-time reflections from our personal encounters with the Lord. In addition to our daily emails, these writings are available on our blog, Facebook, and Twitter. The thoughtful comments and wisdom our followers share each day can help us all in our journeys with God.

Our past devotionals on marriage, wisdom, wise living, fatherhood, and more are available in book form. Visit us at www.wisdomhunters .com.

The National Christian Foundation

Founded in 1982 and based in Atlanta, Georgia, the National Christian Foundation (NCF) is a charitable giving ministry that provides wise giving solutions, mobilizes resources, and inspires biblical generosity with Christian families, advisors, and charities. NCF is currently the ninth-largest US nonprofit, having accepted more than $9 billion in contributions and granted more than $7 billion to more than 40,000 charities. The NCF Giving Fund, or donor-advised fund, allows donors to make charitable contributions and then recommend grants to the charities they care about over time. NCF is also an industry leader in accepting gifts of appreciated assets, such as stocks, real estate, and business interests, which enables donors to save taxes and align their charitable goals with their family, business, estate, and legacy plans. Learn more about NCF at www.ncfgiving.com.

More Great
Harvest House Devotionals
by Boyd Bailey

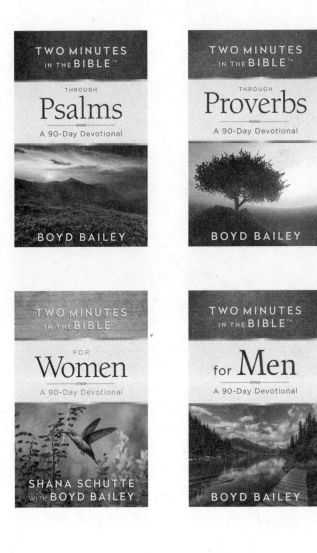

TWO MINUTES
IN THE BIBLE™

THROUGH

Psalms

A 90-Day Devotional

BOYD BAILEY

TWO MINUTES
IN THE BIBLE™

THROUGH

Proverbs

A 90-Day Devotional

BOYD BAILEY

TWO MINUTES
IN THE BIBLE™

FOR

Women

A 90-Day Devotional

SHANA SCHUTTE
WITH BOYD BAILEY

TWO MINUTES
IN THE BIBLE™

for Men

A 90-Day Devotional

BOYD BAILEY

To learn more about Harvest House books and
to read sample chapters, visit our website:

www.harvesthousepublishers.com

HARVEST HOUSE PUBLISHERS
EUGENE, OREGON